Tune-Up Your Small Business

Tune-Up Your Small Business

Improve Operations, Increase Profitability

Dr. Raewyn Sleeman

BEP

BUSINESS EXPERT PRESS

Leader in applied, concise business books

Tune-Up Your Small Business: Improve Operations, Increase Profitability

First published in 2024 by
Business Expert Press, LLC
222 East 46th Street, New York, NY 10017
www.businessexpertpress.com

ISBN-13: 978-1-63742-583-1 (paperback)
ISBN-13: 978-1-63742-584-8 (e-book)

Business Expert Press Portfolio and Project Management Collection

First edition: 2024

10 9 8 7 6 5 4 3 2 1

Description

Tune-Up Your Small Business **is the ideal guide for small business owners who want to achieve their personal and professional goals by making their businesses more successful.**

This book focuses on making regular, small changes that can lead to significant improvements over time. Through stories of small businesses that have grown by following the advice in this book, it offers inspiration and practical advice. Dr. Sleeman provides easy-to-follow steps to help you define what makes your business unique, communicate effectively with your customers, and present your business accurately online.

The book also advises on how to get better by listening to customers, ensuring your team delivers the best service, and discovering what customers are looking to purchase. You will find simple advice on how to price your services and reduce expenses without losing value.

Keywords

small business; business personality; incremental improvements; financial performance; marketing strategy; project management; customer experience; visibility; profitability; cost management; pricing; growth mindset; services marketing

Contents

Preface

In this powerful and insightful book, Dr. Raewyn Sleeman shares her vast expertise in marketing, business strategy, and customer experience to help small business owners unlock their potential and achieve remarkable growth. With a strong background in driving growth across various industries, Dr. Sleeman has developed innovative marketing strategies and enhanced customer experience across digital channels.

Having taught master's level marketing and business courses as a management lecturer, Dr. Sleeman uniquely communicates complex concepts effectively, making the complexity simple. This skill is incredibly close to her heart due to her experience overcoming dyslexia and a speech impediment at an early age.

Her doctorate in Business Administration, focusing on branding (business personality) and innovation in small service companies, equips Dr. Sleeman with a solid strategic thinking and problem-solving foundation. In addition, her dedication to giving back to the community through volunteer work showcases her strong leadership and commitment to social responsibility.

Drawing from her experience as the founder of Stratagease Technology Corporation, cofounder of Nimblwit Marketing Corporation, and various senior roles in marketing and communications, Dr. Sleeman offers readers an invaluable resource for navigating the challenges and opportunities small business owners face.

In this book, you will find practical tools, real-life success stories, and step-by-step project briefs to help you gain from the power of business personality and incremental improvements. Dr. Sleeman's dedication to her craft and passion for helping small businesses thrive is evident on every page. We hope this book inspires you to act and transform your business growth.

Introduction

Welcome to a guide that can transform your small service business into a thriving enterprise even during uncertain times. As a small business owner or manager, you may have made minor service adjustments to increase sales and profit only to find that these efforts don't always result in the financial return you expected or hoped for.

Alexander Den Heijer once said, "When a flower doesn't bloom, you fix the environment that the flower is in, not the flower." This statement holds for small businesses trying to make their mark in today's uncertain and hypercompetitive business environment. The challenge is figuring out what needs fixing to make your business bloom.

As a small business owner, it's no secret that marketing can be overwhelming. With so many options available, it can feel like finding a needle in a haystack or seeing a tree in the forest. Confusing growth strategies is why 9 out of 10 of small businesses fail; half is due to bad marketing.

But what if there was a way to cut through the noise and find what spurs business growth? This book is here to help you do just that. Based on science-backed research, it offers practical advice on the vital marketing tactics small business owners should use to succeed when many people offer similar services or products.

I aim to help you find what needs fixing so you don't waste time learning and failing and start growing. I want you to know exactly what your customers are looking for in your business to make improvements that earn their trust and loyalty. With the insights and strategies in this book, you can.

If you're ready to achieve the goals you started your business for but have limited time, money, and marketing knowledge, this book is for you. Say goodbye to quick short-term fixes and empty silver bullets and hello to a science-based approach to marketing that will help your small business thrive over the long term.

Designed to help you, the small business owner or manager, this book makes the most of your limited time, resources, and expertise. Following the step-by-step guidance, you will learn to effectively prioritize and implement improvements in your business personality, marketing, and continuous innovation efforts.

I have written this guide in plain language, free of jargon, so you can quickly grasp the concepts and put them into practice. In this guide, you'll find five key chapters, each focusing on a different aspect of growing your small service company, with the sixth providing a summary of each chapter:

1. The Power of Business Personality
2. Embracing Change for Growth
3. Visibility for Success
4. Continuous Growth and New Ideas: Unlocking Your Business Potential
5. Maximizing Profitability: Pricing and Cost Management Strategies for Small Businesses
6. Conclusion

Each chapter has actionable advice, simple project management steps, and real-world case studies demonstrating how other small businesses have succeeded in their business personality and improvement efforts.

By following the guidance in this book, you can expect to see at least three main benefits:

1. Reduced waste of time and money on ineffective improvements
2. Greater certainty and clarity on how to achieve your financial performance goals
3. Increased confidence in your ability to implement improvements with limited resources

You'll learn to prioritize improvements based on research and evidence rather than simply copying competitors or relying on guesswork. This way, you can focus on what works for your unique business and achieve your personal and business goals.

This guide is built on a foundation of research and practical experience, combining the latest findings in small business marketing with tried-and-tested project management techniques. As a result, you can trust that the advice provided here is relevant and attainable for small business owners like yourself.

By the time you finish reading this book, you'll have gained valuable insights and practical tools to help your small service company thrive in any business environment. You'll learn how to create a consistent and appealing business personality, adapt to market changes, make your business personality visible to potential customers, continuously improve and innovate your services, and manage pricing and costs effectively.

Ultimately, this book aims to bridge the gap between theoretical marketing knowledge and practical project management techniques, giving you the tools and confidence to achieve your personal and financial goals for your small service business. Following the recommendations in each chapter ensures that your business survives and thrives amid uncertainty and competition.

Now is the time to take control of your small service company's future. Read on to discover how you can make the most of your marketing and business personality efforts and unlock the full potential of your business.

Introduction to Effective Project Management for Small Business Owners

As a small business owner, you wear many hats, and managing projects is an essential skill to ensure success. The good news is that you don't need a degree in project management to achieve your goals. This introduction will provide you with the fundamental principles of effective project management, broken down into plain language and easy-to-follow steps. By applying these principles to the project briefs in this book, you can set yourself and your business up for success. I have weaved these principles into a life cycle within each chapter.

Set clear objectives: Every project starts with a clear goal. What do you want to achieve? Whether creating a business personality, improving the customer experience, or incremental improvements to your services or service delivery, define your objectives to give your project direction and purpose.

Break it down: Divide your project into smaller, manageable tasks. Smaller tasks make the project easier to handle and help you focus on one at a time. Next, list all the activities needed to complete the project and assign each deadline. Each project within this book provides tasks for you to set a deadline based on your resources and availability.

Prioritize: With limited time and resources, it's essential to prioritize tasks based on the immediate benefit to your business. Focus on the tasks shown in each of the project briefs in this book because they will significantly impact achieving your project objectives.

Allocate resources: Identify the resources you'll need to complete each task. Resources may include time, money, equipment, and people. Be realistic about what you can achieve with your available resources and adjust your plan accordingly.

Delegate: As a small business owner, it can be challenging to let go of control, but delegating tasks to your team, external resources, or partners is sometimes crucial for project success. Assign tasks based on each team member's, contractor's, or supplier's strengths and ensure that they understand their responsibilities.

Monitor progress: Regularly review your project's progress to stay on track to meet your goals. Monitoring lets you identify any issues or delays early and adjust as needed.

Communicate: Keep communication open with your team and anyone else involved in the project or impacted by the changes that will occur from a completed project. Provide regular updates on progress, address any concerns, and ensure that everyone has the same current information.

Be flexible: Projects rarely go exactly as planned. Be prepared to adapt and adjust your plan as new information or challenges arise. Embrace change and view it as an opportunity to learn and improve.

Evaluate and learn: Once your project is complete, take the time to review and evaluate the results. What went well? What could you have done better? Then, learn from your experience and apply these insights to future projects.

Celebrate success: Acknowledge your and your team's hard work and celebrate your project's success. Recognition increases morale and encourages a culture of continuous improvement and growth.

Following these 10 principles gives you a solid foundation for effective project management. As you work through the project briefs in this book, remember that practice makes perfect. The more you apply these principles, the more confident and efficient you'll become in managing projects, even with limited time, resources, and budget.

You must embrace flexibility and adaptability to succeed in today's dynamic business landscape. As discussed in this book, being flexible (Principle 8: Entire Lifecycle: Be Flexible) is vital in various aspects covered within these pages. Whether shaping and refining your business personality, embracing change, increasing your company's visibility, fostering continuous growth, or effectively managing costs and pricing, the ability to adjust and adapt based on feedback and changing market dynamics is paramount. Adopting a flexible mindset, you will be better able to navigate challenges, seize opportunities, and achieve long-term success in your small business.

So, get started and embrace the journey of becoming effective at carrying out improvements for the growth of your business. You can succeed in every project with determination, perseverance, and the right mindset.

CHAPTER 1

The Power of Business Personality

In Chapter 1, I'll guide you through the critical aspects of developing a solid business personality for your small business, anchored on the principle of setting clear objectives. We'll start by examining why a strong business personality is essential for financial success in Section 1.1. Here, breaking down tasks and prioritizing efforts come into focus.

In Section 1.2, we go beyond just branding elements such as logos and delve into the holistic view of a business personality, including how it communicates and engages with customers. Practical steps and examples will help you shape an appealing and consistent image.

Section 1.3 features a case study of a small service company that successfully built a distinctive business personality, demonstrating the power of effective task delegation and monitoring progress.

We round off with key takeaways in Section 1.4, emphasizing the principles of communication and flexibility. To assist in implementing these insights, Sections 1.5 through 1.8 offer project briefs designed around developing a business personality that is unique, a promise that matches it, and creating an online presence that reflects your business personality.

By the end of this chapter, you'll be equipped to build a compelling business personality that not only sets you apart but also adapts swiftly to market changes.

1.1 Why Your Business' Personality Matters

As a small business owner, having a solid business personality is essential. Your business personality is like the personality of your business as if it was a person. It's about how your business talks, acts, looks, sounds, and interacts with customers. Your business personality affects how customers see your business and influence their decision to choose your services and products over others.

When a business focuses on building a strong brand or focus on branding, it's called business personality. Research shows that having a robust business personality can help a company perform better and be more attractive. For example, business personality (branding orientation) accounts for 20 percent of the total variability (difference) in company financial performance. In addition, as shown in Figure 1.1, businesses that strongly agree with business personality practices have 2.5 times better financial performance than those who

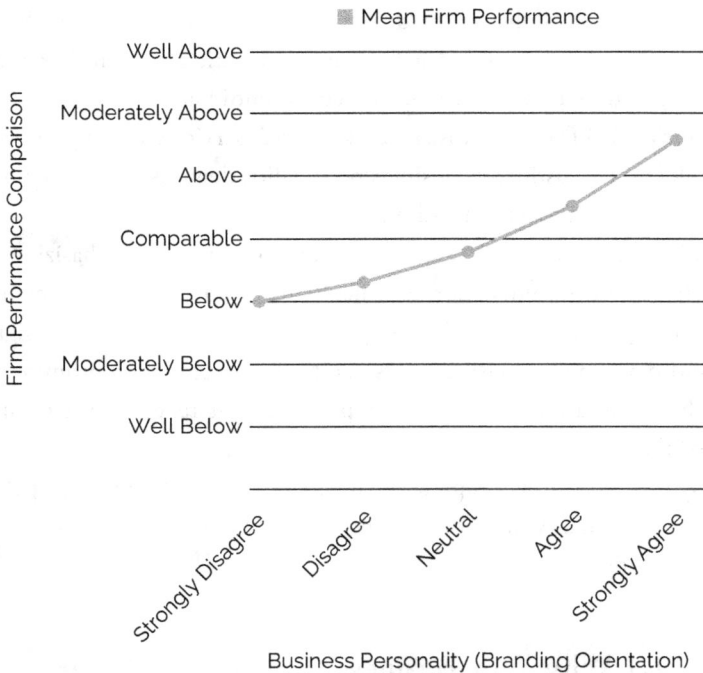

> Business personality (branding orientation) accounts for 20 percent of the total variability (difference) in company financial performance.

Figure 1.1 Impact of business personality practices (branding orientation) on financial performance compared to competitors in small service firms

Source: Dr. Raewyn Sleeman, DBA Thesis 2020.

strongly disagree. Agreement means companies that focus on building a strong personality are much more likely to succeed than those that don't.

Business personality is essential for small businesses since it makes your business credible and trustworthy with potential customers. A company with a strong personality conveys that it is professional, established, and trustworthy. A strong business personality can be vital for newer or smaller companies that may not have a long track record or established reputation.

Another benefit of having a strong business personality is that it helps your business be noticed in a crowded marketplace. Customers are often overwhelmed with choices when many people offer similar products or services, and a strong business personality can help show customers why they should choose your business. Differentiating your business could mean having a unique business personality, such as a distinctive logo or color scheme, or having a strong business personality voice that is attractive to customers. For example, a coffee shop that has a fun and quirky business personality voice might stand out from more traditional coffee shops in the area.

A strong business personality can also help businesses build a loyal customer base. When customers feel strongly connected to a business personality, they are more likely to become repeat customers and recommend the company to others. Repeat customers can help companies save on marketing and advertising costs, as they can rely on word-of-mouth referrals from satisfied customers.

A solid business personality can also help businesses find and keep top people. When a business has a strong character and a positive reputation, it can be easier to attract the best-fit employees interested in working for a company with a strong mission and values. Plus, when employees feel proud to be associated with a strong business personality, they are more likely to be motivated and engaged in their work.

Finally, having a strong business personality can help businesses weather difficult times or crises. When a company has a strong personality and a loyal customer base, it can be easier to recover from setbacks or negative publicity. In addition, customers who feel a strong connection to a business personality are more likely to forgive mistakes or missteps and may even be more likely to continue to use the business during challenging times.

Overall, having a strong business personality is essential for small businesses that want to succeed when many people offer similar services or products. A strong business personality can help establish credibility and trust with customers, separate your company from competitors, build a loyal customer base, attract top talent, and weather difficult times or crises. As a result, you can improve your chances of success and achieve your goals by prioritizing business personality activities and focusing on building a solid business personality.

Setting clear objectives is crucial to ensure that your business personality will achieve your goals. As we discussed earlier, building a strong business personality involves creating a distinct identity for your business that people who buy from your business can easily recognize. Distinction elements include a logo, catchy slogan, color scheme, or similar tone of voice and language in social media posts. However, without clear objectives, these efforts might lack direction and purpose. Setting specific, measurable goals for your business personality is essential. For example, you could aim to increase customer recognition of your logo by a certain percentage or create a consistent voice (style of speaking) across your social media, e-mails, and ads. Clear objectives act as a roadmap, helping you shape your business personality to support and propel you toward achieving your business and personal goals.

Developing a strong online presence via your website and social media pages helps you reach more customers and build your business personality. Creating relevant and valuable content for people who buy your services, engaging with customers, and responding to their feedback, are crucial elements of building a robust online presence.

Understanding people who buy your services and what they value is essential for tailoring your business personality activities to be compelling to them. In addition, investing in advertising and other marketing activities that are most effective in reaching people who buy your services is also crucial.

Meeting your promised customer experience and positive reviews help you build trust and customer loyalty. In addition, responding quickly to customer inquiries and complaints can help you stand out from your competitors.

When many people sell the same type of products or services, having a solid business personality can make a significant difference in the success of your business. By investing time and resources into your business personality, you can show why people should pick your business over others and attract potential customers. However, when many people sell the same type of product or services, it may be necessary to prioritize other aspects of your business, such as improving the quality of your products or services, or incremental innovation, to stay relevant.

Overall, building a strong business personality is essential for small business success. Businesses can attract more customers who are loyal and gain a financial advantage by focusing on business personality and prioritizing impactful business personality activities.

After a comprehensive exploration of why business personality matters for small businesses, it's clear that establishing a strong and distinct personality can significantly impact your business. Distinction involves various components, such as creating a memorable logo, a distinctive voice, and a recognizable company image. However, the wealth of considerations can seem daunting at first.

That's where the principle of breaking tasks down comes into play. Consider each facet of your business personality as a task—developing a logo, creating your business voice, establishing an online presence, enhancing customer experience, and so on. This way, it becomes more manageable, and you can focus on each task individually to ensure that it matches your overall business personality.

Moreover, as it is crucial to direct your efforts to the most critical aspects when many people offer similar services or products, it brings us to the principle of prioritizing. Here, it would be worthwhile to identify the critical business personality aspects that will make the most significant difference in your business success. By prioritizing these crucial aspects, you can efficiently use your resources and make your business personality efforts more impactful.

In conclusion, breaking tasks down and prioritizing are powerful strategies that make building a solid business personality manageable and effective. They ensure that you can navigate the journey toward a strong business personality without being overwhelmed and that your efforts directly contribute to your business's financial advantage.

1.2 Creating and Maintaining a Consistent Business Personality

As discussed in Section 1.1, a strong business personality is essential for business success. However, it's not enough to have a strong business personality; you also need to maintain a consistent one. Consistency is critical to building customer trust while creating a memorable business personality that stands out.

Creating a consistent business personality starts with defining your businesses' values and mission. These should align with your business goals and be communicated to all employees to ensure that everyone has the same information. For example, if your business values customer experience, everything your business does, from how you answer the phone to the language used in your marketing materials, should reflect that value.

Suppose you are a local restaurant focusing on sustainability and supporting local farmers. You have defined your business personality values as promoting sustainable food practices and using locally sourced ingredients. Your values should be reflected in your menu, which changes based on the season and availability of local produce, and in your marketing, materials highlighting your commitment to sustainability. In addition, you train your employees to communicate this value to customers and provide information about the local farms and producers you work with.

Suppose you are a small online clothing boutique that values inclusivity and body positivity. You have defined your business personality mission as providing fashionable and affordable clothing for all body types and sizes. Reflect your mission in your product offerings, which range from XS to 3XL, and in your marketing materials that feature models of different sizes and body types. You will also train your employees to communicate this value to customers and provide personalized recommendations based on individual body types and preferences.

One way to maintain consistency is to create a business personality style guide. This guide should include details about your logo, color scheme, font, and other visual elements used in your marketing materials. It should also have guidelines for the tone of voice and language used in all customer communications, from e-mails to social media posts.

A small catering company could benefit from creating a consistent look and feel for its business. Achieved by creating a library with pictures and designs representing the company's unique style. The library can then be a reference guide for all marketing materials, from menus to social media posts, to ensure a cohesive and recognizable business personality picture. A "library" shows the business's personality, including its color scheme, font, images, and other design elements. Here are some specific examples of items to include in a small business's library:

Color palette: A library will include a page showcasing the business personality's color palette, including the specific shades and combinations of colors used in the marketing materials.

Typography: A library will include examples of the fonts used in the business personality's marketing materials, including specific font families, font sizes, and styles. As an example, this book is written using font family Times New Roman, and the font size is 12, and the style is normal.

Imagery: A library will include examples of pictures in the business personality's marketing materials, including photography, illustrations, and graphics. Choosing a specific type of image that will be used anywhere a customer sees them increases the chance they will recognize your company instantly. Include guidelines for the style and tone of the photos and specific guidelines for size and placement. As an example, your style might be pictures of people experiencing your service, the tone of the photos might be full color, black and white, or shades of your logo color.

Design elements: A library will include examples of the design elements used in the business personality's marketing materials, such as patterns, textures, or other graphic elements. Include specific guidelines for how these design elements should be used and combined.

Overall, a library is a helpful tool to ensure consistency in your business's personality across all marketing materials. It provides a clear and concise library that employees can refer to when creating new marketing materials, ensuring that all materials align with your business's personality.

An independent bookstore could benefit from developing a "library" that outlines its business personality, values, and mission. This document can include information on the types of books the store specializes in, the store's unique selling points, and how they want customers to feel when they visit the store. By sharing this information with employees, the bookstore can ensure that everyone can confidently deliver a consistent customer experience.

A small fashion boutique would benefit from creating a "library" outlining the critical design elements of its business personality. The library will include information on the store's preferred color scheme, font, and imagery. By having these elements clearly defined and documented, the boutique can ensure that all marketing materials, from product packaging to social media posts, are consistent and reflect the boutique's unique style.

Another critical aspect of creating a consistent business personality is to ensure that all customer touchpoints are consistent. Touchpoints include everything from your website to your storefront and customer interactions with your employees. For example, if your business is known for its friendly and helpful customer experience, train all employees to reflect that personality in customer interactions.

Consistency in business personality is also essential for businesses with multiple locations or franchises. Each location should have the same business personality materials and follow the same guidelines to maintain consistency and ensure that customers have a consistent experience, no matter which site they visit.

Let's look at a few examples to demonstrate the importance of consistency. For example, Starbucks is known for its consistent business personality, with the same logo, color scheme, and font used in all locations worldwide. This consistency creates a memorable business personality and helps customers easily recognize and trust the business personality. Similarly, Coca-Cola has maintained a consistent business personality for over 100 years, with the same logo and messaging used throughout its history.

On the other hand, businesses that fail to maintain a consistent business personality can confuse customers and harm their reputation. For example, suppose a restaurant has a friendly and welcoming atmosphere. Still, its website and social media pages are dark and uninviting. In that case, it can create confusion and negatively impact customers choosing your business.

In summary, creating and maintaining a consistent business personality is essential for building customer trust and creating a memorable business personality that stands out from the competition. Start by defining your business's personality and breaking down tasks to establish a consistent character. You can ensure that each aspect of your business personality receives the attention it deserves when broken into manageable tasks. Also, it's crucial to prioritize specific elements of your business personality that align with why people buy your products or services. By identifying the key features that are attractive to people who buy from your business and focusing on them, you can strengthen your business personality and create a more impactful connection with your customers. Lastly, by adhering to these principles and maintaining consistency within your business, such as your website, social media, and customer service, you can create a strong and recognizable business personality that customers will remember and trust.

1.3 Success in Action: A Small Service Firm's Business Personality (Cleaning Company)

Small service companies face unique challenges when it comes to business personality. This case study explores the successful business personality of a small cleaning company, providing insights and practical strategies that can help other small service companies build and maintain a strong business personality.

Background of the company: The small service company we will examine is a cleaning company. A business started by a woman who has provided appreciated customer experiences in the hospitality industry for over 16 years. She started her business to provide a level of service she saw was missing in the commercial and residential services industry. Having completed training and certification from Superhost and Service it Right, her business had an advantage over competitors. However, potential customers weren't aware of the company.

Recognizing the need for change: After a few months in business, in 2017, the owner was determined to provide a spotless customer experience for her cleaning customers and wanted her business to have the best chance of success. There were many competitors in the area, and she found she was competing on price, often getting her estimates declined. She wasn't getting the customers she expected to, given her quality of service and customer experience, so she applied for a mentor from a local entrepreneur support association and met me.

Adapting to market changes: To adapt to the changes in the local market, we reviewed her business and the competition around her business to see the areas that would benefit from improvement. The reasons for developing a business personality were identified when reviewing the business to determine what might be stopping customers from using this business that provided excellent cleaning services and an above-standard customer experience. Initially, the company had a logo and social media page that showed pictures of cleaning products and a clean home. Still, there wasn't an evident business personality with images and messages that demonstrated the uniqueness of this company.

The process began with a comprehensive analysis of what customers liked and didn't like about the company and looking to see what other cleaning companies looked like in the area. This review helped identify how this cleaning company was unique and what a natural business personality would be that reflected the business experienced by its current customers and owner.

After my team and I created her new business personality and everything about the company was adapted to the new character—website, social media, vehicle signage, uniform, unique touches—a launch party was held to increase awareness by current and potential customers, followed by regular, consistent social media posts, paid and unpaid.

Results of the company's adaptation: Owing to these changes, the cleaning company had an increase of 1,233 percent in customer website leads and could overachieve its personal and business goals. She was able to attract new customers and retain existing ones by adapting to the changes in the marketplace, which demonstrated to her most profitable customers that her business could meet their needs better than the competition.

New customers experienced exceptional service and "a spotless clean," which her existing customers were used to. This business continued to grow and remained top of mind when it was closed during the pandemic by changing the messaging to be relevant and supportive of business and personal customers' experiences through the Covid pandemic.

The impact of a strong business personality on the cleaning company's performance was significant. The business personality resulted in a dramatic increase in customers and increased loyalty from existing clients. The company also experienced increased revenue and profitability, achieving financial goals within a year. Maintaining the business personality for over five years has increased customer and prospect confidence in the company, with continual new customer requests every week.

Key takeaways for small business owners: First, it's essential to stay aware of the local market, competition changes, and customer and prospect responses to advertising and promotion. Know how vital a strong business personality is and act when results don't achieve your goals.

Second, building a strong business personality and messages can help small businesses stand out from other similar companies, making it easier for the right—most profitable customers—to find them and immediately recognize that it is a company they can trust and rely upon.

Third, being open to changing the business personality of a company—logo, name, pictures, and messaging ensures that you attract new customers and increase revenue. Finally, using social media channels to announce improvements and demonstrate the unique business personality of a company will help small enterprises to reach a wider audience and build awareness and trust with potentially profitable customers. Continuing to prioritize investments in the business personality and monitor customer feedback and the business environment and change pictures and messages as the market changes as it did during the years of the Covid pandemic is also essential.

This case study has highlighted the importance of a successful business personality creation for small service companies. Through this project, the cleaning company built a strong personality for the business that set it apart from its competitors, attracted new customers, and retained existing ones. The business personality process involves understanding what customers like about the established company, defining the personality, developing visual pictures and messages to show the character of the company, and implementing the essence of the company across all aspects of the business, from signs, clothing, interior design and décor, giveaways, promotions, advertisements, social media posts, websites, vehicle signage, equipment, and tools.

By following the strategies and tactics outlined in this case study, you experience the benefits of investing in business personality and see why developing a unique business personality for growth is essential.

One important aspect highlighted in this case is how a small service company effectively allocated resources to create and maintain its business personality. They carefully assigned their budget, time, and people to personality and marketing tactics, ensuring their business personality was nurtured and consistently reflected across all touchpoints. Plus, the role of delegation is emphasized in implementing and executing the strategies to uphold the business personality.

The small service company effectively managed its workload by delegating tasks to competent team members or outsourcing specific responsibilities. The business owner ensured her business personality was effectively implemented. Through these practices, you can achieve long-term success and stand out when many people offer similar services/products by consistently establishing and maintaining your unique business personality.

1.4 The Power of Business Personality: Key Insights and Next Steps

Section 1.1 outlined the importance of business personality for small businesses. In the previous sections, I covered the key elements of building and maintaining a solid business personality, including the benefits of creating and maintaining a consistent business personality and a case study of a successful small service company's business personality creation.

I discussed why a strong business personality matters for your small business and how focusing on business personality activities can positively impact your performance and financial advantage in the future. By prioritizing your business personality efforts, you can improve your financial performance and achieve more significant revenue over other similar small businesses.

I delved into creating and maintaining a consistent business personality, as it is not just about having a logo but also about how you talk, act, and interact with customers. I provided examples and practical steps to build and maintain a consistent business personality that is attractive to people who buy your services. I discussed how to adapt to changes in the business environment to remain relevant.

I showcased the case study of a successful small service company's business personality creation. I highlighted how they implemented an effective business personality to show what's unique about their business and attract loyal customers. I examined their journey from the early stages of business personality to their current success. I provided insights into how you can apply these strategies to your own business.

As a small business owner, it is essential to recognize that a strong business personality is vital for your business's success, even though it can be hard to separate yourself from the character of your business. When you recognize the importance of having a separate and professional business personality consistent across all areas of your business, you can drastically increase trust by current and potential customers, resulting in less work for you and increased revenue and profitability.

Through these sections, I aim to demonstrate that business personality is vital for small businesses and can make the difference between those that thrive and those that do not. By building a solid business personality, you can attract loyal customers, make your business stand out from others, and be seen as relevant as the market changes and you adapt.

Discussing the importance of monitoring progress to ensure that your business personality remains consistent and aligned with your objectives is essential. Regularly assessing and evaluating your efforts allows you to make necessary adjustments and maintain the desired impact of your business personality.

Effective communication also significantly conveys and reinforces your business personality to people involved or purchasing from your business. By delivering your messages consistently across various channels, such as social media, e-mails, and customer service, you establish a strong connection with the people who buy your products and services and strengthen your business personality.

Before progressing, consider diving into the project briefs designed to help you build a compelling business personality and benefits message for your business. Following a structured Start, Plan, Do, Finish approach, these briefs guide you from research to execution.

Project brief 1.5 initiates the journey by focusing on research to differentiate your business. Project brief 1.6 then helps you develop a clear and cohesive business personality, including visual elements such as logos and color schemes. Briefs 1.7 and 1.8 are about making an actionable promise that matches your business personality and ensuring your online presence genuinely reflects your business personality.

Up next, we'll explore how to adapt to change, offering insights to keep your business relevant. By the end of these chapters, you'll have the tools and insights to systematically and effectively build a business personality that resonates with people who will buy your products or services.

1.5 Start: Research to Differentiate Your Business Personality

As a small business owner, understanding your customers' preferences and the unique aspects of your business personality that sets you apart from competitors is critical. This project brief guides you through a process of market research aimed at achieving these crucial insights.

In this brief, we explore how to conduct effective market research, develop a relevant customer survey, and apply the data gained to set your business personality as different from the rest.

Objectives

Your research objective for this project is to identify ways to demonstrate your business personality uniqueness using customer feedback.

Scope

- Reviewing customer feedback online
- Developing a simple online survey
- Sharing the survey with current customers
- Analyzing the data
- Implementing changes based on the findings

Deliverables

- Collection and review of at least 50 customer feedbacks
- Creation and distribution of a simple online survey
- Analysis of customer feedback
- Actionable insights and implementation plan based on findings

Timeline

- Reviewing feedback: One week
- Developing and sharing survey: One week
- Gathering and analyzing data: Two weeks
- Implementing changes based on results: Variable

Resources

- Online tools such as Google Forms, SurveyMonkey, and 1000minds
- Social media platforms for sharing surveys
- Charts or graphs for data visualization
- Incentives to encourage customer participation

Risks and Challenges

- Gathering sufficient feedback to form a representative sample
- Ensuring meaningful participation through incentives
- Analyzing and correctly interpreting data
- Implementing changes based on insights gained

Key Stakeholders (People Who Care About What Your Business Does)

- Business owner
- Marketing person—internal or external
- Customers

Step 1: Recognize the Need to Show Customers You're Different

Recognize the need to make your business stand out from others through comprehensive market research. A crucial part of this process is to review customer feedback online, both positive and negative. Ensure that you have at least 50 customer feedback instances for a representative and reliable sample. Too few feedback experiences may result in a business personality that does not match the expectations of paying customers. By comprehensively understanding customer perspectives, you will be able to associate your business personality with your customers' expectations.

Step 2: Communicate With People Who Care About Your Business

Communication with key stakeholders is vital. Your key stakeholders are anyone who cares about what your business does. For this project, they are your staff and your customers. Use any available channels to engage them in this process. Your channels may be to communicate via social media, e-mail, telephone, or face-to-face interactions, depending on which you use now. The goal is to ensure that they understand the project's objective and are actively involved in providing the feedback needed for market research. The method of communication is less important than the quality and quantity of the feedback collected. So, use whatever means are most accessible and efficient to make this important discussion and feedback happen.

Step 3: Involve Team

Involve your team in developing the survey using online survey tools. Keep your survey short and simple, focusing on questions to help achieve your research objectives. For example:

- How do you think our company is different from our competitors? (Or other companies you have used that provide the same services)
- What makes our business stand out or different from the rest?
- What words come to mind if you were to describe the personality of our business to someone else as if it was a person?
- What do you like least about your experience with our company?
- What do you like most about your experience with our company?

Step 4: Provide Resources and Training

Give your team what they need, including online survey tools. Train them to use these tools and interpret survey data effectively. Once the survey is ready, distribute it through various channels such as social media, e-mail, or your website. Offer incentives, such as products or complementary services, to encourage customer participation.

Step 5: Refine and Adjust as Necessary

After getting feedback from customers, look for common points and trends. Use easy-to-understand charts or graphs to see and understand what the data is telling you. For example, if customers value customer experience over price, you could show how you are different by offering a relevant customer experience. If customers perceive your business personality as outdated compared to competitors, consider updating your business personality and messaging.

Step 6: Celebrate Success and Learn From Failure

Celebrate the insights gained and strategies for implementing changes based on the findings. Learn from any challenges faced during the process to improve future research.

Tips

- Keep your survey short and simple; use existing wording and questions provided in survey tools rather than writing your own unless you have market research experience.
- Offer incentives to encourage participation.
- Use online tools to save time and money.
- Create a chart or graph of your collected information with simple charts or graphs to see trends.
- Act based on your research findings; update your business personality and messaging to better appeal to people who buy your services if necessary.

By following these steps and researching, you will have information about what your customers prefer to clarify how your business differs from competitors.

1.6 Plan: Developing a Clear Business Personality

The development of a clear and consistent business personality is of critical importance. It is a cornerstone for your marketing strategy, effectively communicating your business' values and unique offerings to customers. Your business personality is how your business behaves, speaks, and communicates with customers. Your business personality is made up of visual elements that reflect the uniqueness of your company for customers to recognize and remember your business based on the visual clues you present, such as your logo icon, color palette, and fonts.

Therefore, this project aims to guide establishing a strong business personality that allows small businesses to show their uniqueness compared to similar companies to build trust with potential customers.

In this brief, we explore the step-by-step process of developing a clear business personality, from defining the business tone, voice, and style, to selecting the appropriate visual elements such as colors and fonts, and finally, creating a memorable and representative logo.

Objectives

Developing a personality that effectively communicates my business's unique offerings and values to customers, which helps attract and keep customers.

Scope

- Defining the business personality
- Selection of colors that align with the business personality
- Choosing appropriate fonts that reflect the business personality
- Creating a logo that represents the business personality
- Ensuring consistency across all elements of the business personality

Deliverables

- A clear definition of the business personality
- A defined color scheme representing the business personality
- A chosen font style aligning with the business personality
- A representative and easily recognizable logo
- A guide to maintaining consistency in the business personality

Timeline

- Define your business personality (one to two weeks)
- Choose your business personality colors (one week)
- Select your business personality fonts (one week)
- Create a logo (one week)
- Maintain consistency (ongoing)

Resources

- Customer feedback (from Reviews or Research, see Section 1.5)
- Tools to develop the tone of voice and style (Grammarly, Hemingway, CopyLime)
- Color palette generators and design books for color scheme inspiration
- Online font collections for font selection inspiration
- High-quality pictures and graphics for logo design

Risks and Challenges

- Failure to effectively define the business personality
- Inconsistency in the application of business personality across different channels
- Choosing colors, fonts, and logos that do not align with the business personality

Key Stakeholders

- Business owner(s)
- Design team (if available)
- Customers

Step 1: Recognize the Need for a Business Personality

You must recognize that developing a clear business personality separates you from competitors, driving customer attraction and retention. Begin with defining your business personality's tone, voice, and style.

Define your business personality

Your business personality is the set of human characteristics that your business personality exhibits. Keep your business personality identity simple and focused.

To develop your business personality, you need to define your business personality's tone, voice, and style. Start by asking yourself the following questions:

- What did customers say in the survey or what do customers say they like and dislike about my business in online reviews?
- How do you want your business personality perceived by your customers?
- What adjectives would you use to describe your business personality?
- What values does your business personality stand for?
- What emotions do you want your business personality to evoke in your customers?

Once you have answers to these questions, you can develop your business personality's tone of voice and style. Your tone of voice is how your business personality communicates with your customers, and your style is the visual representation of your business personality.

To help you develop your tone of voice and style, you can use the following tools:

- Grammarly: Grammarly is a free writing assistant that helps you improve your grammar and spelling.

- Hemingway: Hemingway is a free online editor that helps you improve your writing and readability.
- CopyLime: CopyLime is a free online editor that helps you write more engaging and responsive information.

Colors

The next step in creating a business personality is to choose your business personality colors. Use the same ones everywhere—your website, social media pages, marketing materials, internal and external physical stores, trade shows, stands, signage, flyers, postcards, and business cards. Choose colors that reflect your business personality identity and are easy to view. Use a maximum of three colors to keep it simple for customers.

Choose a color scheme: The colors you choose for your business personality can significantly impact how people perceive your company. For example, suppose your business provides luxury spa services. In that case, you might choose colors such as gold and purple to convey a sense of elegance and sophistication. To select a color scheme, consider your business's personality and the colors that best represent it. You can also look at color palettes online or in design books for inspiration.

Here are some examples of the meaning of colors and the most common colors used by different business industries:

Red: This color is often associated with excitement, passion, and energy. It is commonly used by businesses in the food, entertainment, and retail industries, promoting urgency and appetite.

Blue: Blue is associated with professionalism, loyalty, and trust. It is commonly used by businesses in the technology, finance, and health care industries, as it can create a sense of security and reliability.

Green: Green is associated with health, growth, and nature. It is used by businesses in the organic food, environmental, and wellness industries for a sense of vitality and freshness.

Yellow: Yellow is often associated with optimism, creativity, and warmth. It is commonly used by businesses in the hospitality, entertainment, and retail industries, as it can create a sense of happiness and friendliness.

Purple: This color is often associated with luxury, royalty, and creativity. It is commonly used by businesses in the beauty, fashion, and entertainment industries, as it can convey a sense of sophistication and glamor.

When choosing a color scheme for your business, it's essential to consider the meanings associated with each color and how they align with your business's personality and values. It's also helpful to look at what colors are commonly used in your industry, as this can create a sense of familiarity and help you stand out from competitors. You can find inspiration for color schemes online or in design books, and even use color palette generators to help you select complementary colors.

An example for a restaurant:

The color scheme might include warm colors such as red and orange to stimulate appetite.

Fonts

The next step in creating a business personality is to choose your business personality fonts. These should be the same for everything, including your website, social media posts, marketing materials, signage, flyers, uniforms, vehicle decals, and window displays. Choose fonts that reflect your business personality identity and are easily read and comprehended with the colors chosen in the previous step.

The font you choose for your logo and website can also significantly impact how people perceive your business personality. For example, if your business provides legal services, choose a traditional font that is easy to read, such as Times New Roman. To select a font, consider your business's personality and what font best represents it. You can also look at font collections online to get inspiration. For example, do not use Comic Sans for any part of your business personality to avoid looking immature or childish.

Here is an example for a fitness studio:

A fitness studio's font choice might be a strong and bold serif font to convey strength and power. Try Georgia, Baskerville, or Times New Roman.

Logo

The next step to creating a business personality is to create a logo that reflects your business personality.

Choose an icon that reflects your business: Your company's logo needs to be immediately recognizable by prospects. A recognizable logo is harder for some businesses than others. For example, suppose your business provides multiple products or product categories. In that case, it will be challenging to choose one image for its logo, as will companies that provide some services that don't have imagery that makes it easily recognizable.

Your logo should be straightforward, easy to recognize, and reflect what your business provides so it's instantly obvious.

Tips

- Use high-quality pictures and graphics to maintain a professional appearance.
- Choose imagery and graphics that reflect your business personality identity and messaging.
- Choose a specific image type for your business—will it be photographs or illustrations? Will they have a solid color background or natural? Choosing a color from your business personality and using it repeatedly will increase awareness of your business whenever someone sees it. But again, it's essential to choose a specific style and be consistent.

An Example for a Legal Services Company

A legal company's business personality might include a logo that incorporates a symbol of justice, such as a scale, gavel, or courthouse.

It's important to note that while all these visual elements are different, they should all work together to create a cohesive and consistent business personality for the business.

The logo, color scheme, and font choice should reflect the business's personality and values and be used consistently across all marketing materials.

Maintain Consistency

Avoid changing your business personality too often, if at all, as it can confuse customers and potentially lead to losing trust in your business. Instead, ensure that any changes align with your business personality's messaging and values.

Developing an evident business personality is essential for you if you want to show how your business differs from similar companies to attract the right customers. By defining your business personality, keeping it consistent, and communicating it effectively, you can build a strong business personality that is attractive to current and new customers.

Step 2: Communicate With Key Stakeholders

Once you've defined your business personality, you must share it with the people who help your business function, such as your employees, contractors, and suppliers. Share because your business personality isn't just a statement; it's a commitment to your customers and should change how you operate.

Let's say, for instance, you run a café, and your new business personality promise includes only using locally sourced ingredients. Sourcing ingredients locally is an excellent step toward supporting your community and providing fresh, quality food to your customers. But this will affect your relationship with suppliers.

First, you'd need to talk to your current suppliers. You'd tell them about the change in your business's direction and what it means for them. If they can't provide locally sourced goods, you'll need to transition to a supplier who can. Remember, when communicating this change, it's essential to be clear about why you're doing it (the purpose), how you plan on making the change (the process), and what you hope to achieve (the expected outcomes). This way, everyone in your business understands what's happening and why.

Next, you'd share your new promise with your employees and contractors. After all, they're the ones who will be implementing this promise day in and day out. Suppose your staff knows and understands your business personality. In that case, they can better deliver on that promise and create a consistent customer experience.

So, to recap, after creating your business personality, communicate it to everyone involved in your business. Be clear about why you're making changes, how you plan on implementing them, and what you hope to achieve. Communicating will help everyone understand the new direction of your business and how it can contribute to its success.

Step 3: Involve Team

Your team's insights and inputs are valuable in defining and developing your business personality if they have experience creating one for a successful company. If they have that experience, involve them. For team members who don't have expertise branding a company like yours, while it's essential to communicate the changes with your team, if you have one, remember that it's always the collective profitable customer's opinion that matters most because, without them, your company doesn't exist. Avoid making changes based on personal views that aren't reflective of the needs of your business from your most profitable customers.

Avoid making changes based on the opinions of people who don't understand the psychology behind why customers buy from your company, even though they want to get involved and are well-meaning in their views. While everyone has the right to share their opinion, changing the business personality based on personal goals and ambitions should be avoided so you don't alienate customers or become irrelevant.

Focus on why your business started in the first place and what the need was in the market you were solving. If you veer too far from why customers choose your business, they will switch to your competitors. Beware of incorporating any current cultural trends into your business personality so that customers continue to find you for the need they have that your products or services solve.

Step 4: Provide Resources and Training

When you're ready to bring your business personality to life, you must equip yourself and any team members with the right tools and skills. These resources can help you consistently communicate your promise through your company's visual and verbal style.

For instance, tools for developing tone of voice and style can help you ensure that your written communications align with your promise. An online tool might guide you through selecting words and phrases that fit your company's personality. Color palette generators and design books can inspire your company's visual style. They can help you choose colors that reflect the feeling you want to convey—for example, calming blues for a yoga studio or vibrant oranges for a fast-paced delivery service. Online font collections offer a wide range of typefaces that can complement your visual style. At the same time, high-quality graphics can make your communications more engaging.

Remember, it's not enough just to have these tools—you need to know how to use them effectively. Don't worry if you're not a design whiz or a wordsmith. Online training and creation tools are available, often free, or cheap. Websites such as YouTube, Coursera, or Udemy offer courses on everything from graphic design to copywriting. Artificial intelligence (AI) tools provide creative images and copy by answering a few questions.

When using AI, it's essential to know that the answers you get from the tools are only as good as your knowledge of what you need—and that starts with understanding the strategy that is right for your unique business; if you aren't sure, get an expert's suggestion for the strategy you can use for AI tools on your own. With some time and practice, you'll soon be able to use these tools to communicate your business personality clearly and consistently everywhere customers might see your business—online and in real life.

Step 5: Celebrate Success and Learn From Failure

Congratulations on shaping a unique business personality for your enterprise! This step is a milestone in defining your company's uniqueness. Acknowledging and celebrating this achievement is important because it represents the hard work and thoughtful consideration you've put into understanding your customers' needs. This celebration could be as simple as sharing your excitement with your team or taking a moment to appreciate your hard work.

But remember, it's okay if things don't turn out perfectly the first time. Maybe your initial business personality isn't as attractive to customers as you'd hoped, or your communication efforts need tweaking. It's essential to see these not as failures but as opportunities for learning and growth. Use these instances as lessons to refine your approach. Ask for customer feedback, monitor customer engagement, and use these insights to make necessary adjustments.

The journey to crafting and communicating your business personality is a continual process of trial, learning, and refining. The key is to remain open to change and always keep the needs and preferences of your customers at the forefront. This way, you'll continue to build a robust and appealing business personality that your customers trust and value.

1.7 Do: Developing Your Business Personality Promise

Defining and communicating your unique business personality promise is vital when many people sell similar products or services. This promise is what customers can expect from your service, directly affecting your reputation and customer loyalty. It helps attract more right people for your business, ensuring they appreciate and value your services.

In this brief, we explore how to define your business personality promise and provide you with practical examples across various industries. This project will assist you in creating a unique and impactful promise that rings true with your most profitable customers.

Objectives

The primary objective of this brief is to empower you, a small business owner, to formulate your own compelling business personality promise, thereby strengthening your business personality and enhancing customer loyalty.

Scope

This project brief will cover the following:

- Explanation of the business personality promise and its importance
- A detailed breakdown of the business personality promise Formula

- Practical examples of business personality promises in various industries
- Tips for effective communication of your business personality promise

Deliverables

By the end of this project brief, you will:

- Understand the concept and importance of a business personality promise
- Be able to craft your own business personality promise using the provided formula and examples
- Learn how to communicate your promise across various channels effectively

Timeline

Given this project brief's compact and focused nature, understanding, and applying the concepts should take approximately one week.

Resources

Apart from this guide and your understanding of your business and customers, no additional resources are required. Tools such as Snappa will help create visual representations of your business personality promise.

Risks and Challenges

- Difficulty in clearly defining the most profitable customer type
- Struggling to articulate a clear and concise business personality promise
- Ensuring consistency in communicating the promise across different channels

Key Stakeholders

- You, as the business owner
- Your most profitable customers

- Any employees or team members involved in customer service or communication roles

Step 1: Create Your Business Personality Promise

Your business personality promise is a statement that tells customers the benefits they can expect from your business. It is a promise you make to your customers about what they will experience when they do business with you.

Use the following formula and the example to define your business personality promise. You may have more than one type of customer, so start with the customers who give your business the most profit. It's essential to create a promise based on your most profitable customers. You attract more people who look like this and ensure that you find the right people for your business who will appreciate and value your services. First, write the most profitable customers' problem in terms of the reason they use your service—second, then define what (benefit) they want from your service—and third, why they want that benefit, that is,

Business personality promise formula:

Service – [1][customer problem descriptor] + [2][what they want] + [3][why they want it]

Vet: Busy pet owners who want a reliable and caring veterinarian for their furry family members.

Business personality promise: "We promise to provide top-notch veterinary care with a compassionate and personalized approach, giving you peace of mind that your pets are in good hands."
Example: "Paws & Claws Veterinary Clinic"

This example helps you understand how to create a business personality promise for your small business. Remember to use simple, straightforward language to communicate your business personality promise to your customers.

Be customer-focused and consistently deliver on your commitment to building customer trust.

Step 2: Communicate With Key Stakeholders

Once you have crafted your business personality promise, communicating it effectively to all your key stakeholders, particularly your customers, is crucial. For example, you own a bakery, and your promise is "We promise to provide you with the freshest, most delicious baked goods, made with love and care from locally sourced ingredients, bringing a taste of home to your table every time." You could highlight this promise on your website, store signage, product packaging, advertising material, and flyers you mail to your local community. Remember to use straightforward language, focusing on the benefits your customers will experience.

Social media pages are helpful for sharing your promise. Let's consider you're a personal trainer whose promise is "We promise to provide a motivating and challenging workout experience with knowledgeable and supportive trainers who help you achieve your fitness goals." Share client success stories, workout snippets, nutritional tips, and motivational posts that reflect your promise on your social media channels. Always keep your messaging consistent, ensuring every communication reinforces your business personality promise. Consistency creates trust and fosters a strong and loyal customer base.

Step 3: Involve Your Team

Involving your team in delivering your business's personality promise is not just good practice; it's essential. Let's consider a local restaurant, for instance. The owner decides on a promise of "offering a warm, home-like dining experience with top-quality local ingredients." But the waitstaff isn't trained to deliver this promise. They continue to operate as before, not realizing the importance of making customers feel at home. Over time, they might feel overlooked and frustrated because they are not being trained on the restaurant's personality, even though they are vital in delivering it.

On the other hand, let's consider a small retail clothing store where the owner has promised: "provide personalized, trend-driven style advice for every customer." Suppose the sales associates aren't trained to deliver this promise. In that case, they may not understand the importance of their role in offering style advice, leading to unsatisfied customers and demotivated employees. Don't overlook employees, especially those interacting with customers, because they are invaluable in delivering the experience customers expect from your promises.

Involving your team doesn't mean giving them control over the business personality promise. It's about gathering insights and feedback from their experiences and interactions with customers and then training them on delivering the completed promise. For instance, your bakery staff might tell you that customers often compliment the freshness of your baked goods. You can use this insight to reinforce the freshness aspect of your promise. Or your gym trainers might tell you that clients appreciate their personalized fitness plans, which can become a central part of your promise. By actively including your team in collecting customer insights, you're making them feel valued and engaged and strengthening the effectiveness and authenticity of your business personality promise. After all, they are the ones who deliver this promise to your customers each day.

Step 4: Provide Resources and Training

In simple terms, think of your business personality promise as a clear message that tells your customers what to expect from your services. This message must remain the same everywhere your customers interact with your business, whether online—website, social pages, or offline—physical store, delivery people. Everyone involved in your company should know and understand your promise.

Let's say you own a flower shop. Your business personality promise is "We promise to provide the freshest flowers, handpicked and arranged with love and creativity, adding a touch of beauty to your special moments." You should inform everyone, be it your employees, the person who manages your website, or even the company that handles your social media, about this promise. They all should know how to communicate this promise to customers.

To help them understand, you could hold a meeting or a training session where you explain what this promise means and how to deliver it. Ensure that they know this promise should be the same everywhere: on your social media pages, website, or in person at your shop. This way, your customers always see the same message, which helps them trust your business more. After all, consistency builds trust, which is vital for your business's success.

Step 5: Refine and Adjust as Necessary

After communicating your business personality promise, it's vital to remain attentive to how your customers respond. You might have created a compelling promise today, but business environments constantly change. Competition, technological advancements, and evolving customer needs can impact how well your promise matches customers' needs over time. That said, avoid making swift changes based on isolated feedback or minor shifts in market trends. Consistency in your positioning is vital to maintain customer trust and loyalty.

It's like steering a ship—you wouldn't drastically change course based on a single gust of wind. In the same way, don't rush to alter your promise because of a few comments from customers or even family and friends. Your guide to change should be a noticeable trend among loyal and profitable customers. If they start leaving your business, it may indicate that your promise isn't as attractive as it used to be.

However, be cautious about making frequent changes in response to every new trend. Doing so can confuse your customers, making them question if you truly understand your business. Following all trends causes customer uncertainty leading to a loss of trust, affecting their overall experience. Imagine going to your favorite restaurant only to find they've changed their menu every other week—it would likely leave you confused and less inclined to return. Likewise, your customers must trust that you'll consistently deliver the experience promised. Hence, refine your promise only when necessary, ensuring it remains relevant to your business personality.

Step 6: Celebrate Success and Learn From Failure

In communicating your business personality promise, there will be successes and setbacks. Both offer valuable lessons and should be recognized appropriately. Celebrating your victories is a great way to motivate your-self and any team members you may have. If a customer leaves a positive review that aligns perfectly with your promise, share it on your business's social media pages. Sharing encourages your team and reaffirms your commitment to other customers.

Learning from failures is equally important. Maybe a customer's feedback suggests their experience did not meet your promise. Instead of feeling disheartened, see this as an opportunity to improve. You could respond by apologizing, correcting the issue, and reassuring the customer that you're committed to fulfilling your promise. Responding shows your dedication to your pledge and helps to rebuild trust.

Using tools to enhance your communication efforts can be very bene-ficial. For instance, with Snappa or Canva, you can create visually appeal-ing graphics to share your business personality promise. These could include image banners for your website or image posts for your social media pages. Similarly, a social media management tool can help you schedule posts, track engagement, and manage your online presence more efficiently. These tools require no technical or design skills, making them perfect for anyone new to marketing.

1.8 Finish: Creating an Online Presence That Accurately Reflects Your Business's Personality

In the digital era, creating an online presence that accurately reflects a business's personality is critical for the growth and success of any business. A strong, cohesive, and easily identifiable online presence can improve company recognition, enhance customer trust, and significantly increase conversion rates.

After you've designed your business personality, it's time to update or create your online presence with the style guide. Your online presence should be easy to navigate, visually appealing, and accurately reflect your business's personality.

In this brief, we explore the importance of designing an online pres-ence that mirrors your business's personality and provides a comprehen-sive guide on effectively achieving this goal.

Objectives

This project's primary objective is to guide you through creating or updating your online presence to accurately represent your business's personality to be compelling to people who buy from your company.

Scope

- Building an effective website with essential elements
- Strategically using social media platforms
- Using Google My Business and other mapping services
- Exploring additional tools and resources to enhance online presence

Deliverables

- A comprehensive guide for designing a business website
- A strategy for effective use of different social media platforms
- A walkthrough for using Google My Business and other mapping services
- A list of additional tools and resources for creating a logo and website

Timeline

- Weeks 1 to 2: Developing the website design guide
- Weeks 3 to 4: Crafting the social media strategy
- Week 5: Exploring Google My Business and other mapping services
- Week 6: Compiling a list of additional tools and resources
- Week 7: Review and finalization

Resources

- Expert in web design and development, or website tool that creates the website for you using AI, or get started with initial advice in this project

- Social media strategist, or get started with initial advice on this project
- Digital marketing expert, or get started with initial advice on this project
- Graphic designer, or get started with initial advice on this project

Risks and Challenges

- Difficulty in defining a business's personality
- Creating a cohesive design that reflects the business's personality across different platforms
- Staying up-to-date with changes in social media algorithms and user behavior
- Maintaining a consistent and engaging online presence

Key Stakeholders

- Business owners
- Marketing person—internal or external, or use tools available such as Snappa
- A web development team or use website tools such as WIX, GoDaddy, or Shopify
- Social media team, or use tools available such as Hootsuite or Canva

Step 1: Recognize Online Essentials

When designing your online presence, it's important to include the essential elements to help your visitors find the information they need to act. For example, suppose your business provides event planning services. In that case, your online presence might include pictures of elegant events and a color scheme that reflects a sense of celebration. It's also essential to complete the details that search engines seek from your online presence, so people can easily find your company when searching for your products or services.

Website Essentials

Navigation menu: Make sure your website has a straightforward and easy-to-use navigation menu, so visitors can quickly find what they're looking for.

Contact information: Include your business's phone, e-mail, physical address, and open or contactable times, so visitors can quickly contact you.

About Us page: This page should provide information about your business, such as your mission, history, and team members, so visitors can get to know your business better.

Products & Services page: Provide detailed information about your products or services, including pricing, features, and benefits.

Testimonials or reviews: Including customer testimonials or reviews builds trust and legitimacy with potential customers.

Location mapping: Include a map for directions to your business if it's a physical business or you provide services or products within a specific geographic area.

Social Media Essentials

It's necessary to have a presence online where your most profitable customers hang out.

Choose to spend time for your business on the social media platforms that match what your current customers look like; see which of the following ones they match with. Using the right platforms may mean changing the channels you promote your business, so that your business is where your most profitable customers are looking for services like yours. For example, use Facebook if your profitable customers match the profile of most common users.

Facebook
Predominant age: 25 to 34
Preferred business communication: Direct messaging, posts, ads
Common interests: Family, friends, entertainment, news
Gender: Male and female

Life stage: Married with children, single, married

Lifestyle: Socializing, family-oriented

Needs of consumers using the platform: Information about products and services, customer service

Google My Business (+Other Mapping Companies)

As a small business owner, you should have a Google My Business account, which is free. Use the minimum information to include in your Google My Business account or other mapping site listings shown as follows:

- Accurate business name, address, and phone number
- Business hours
- Website URL
- Photos of the business, products, and services
- Business description—use your business personality messaging and promise
- Customer reviews and ratings
- Categories that describe the business
- Additional details such as accepted payment methods, parking, and accessibility information

While Google Maps is the most popular and widely used mapping search engine globally, you must consider other options that may be more popular in your region or country. Claiming and optimizing your listings on these mapping sites can significantly improve your online visibility and attract more local customers.

Here are the top five global mapping search engines you should consider depending on your location:

Google Maps
Apple Maps
Bing Maps
Here WeGo
OpenStreetMap

Step 2: Communicate Your Online Presence

Once you've put in the effort to create or enhance your online presence, it's time to spread the word about it. Remember, having a fantastic website or a well-managed social media page is not enough. Letting customers, prospects, and employees know about your online improvements or additions is equally essential.

Imagine you've set up a Google My Business account and added a map link to your website for easy navigation. It's now essential to tell everyone that finding your business has become easier than ever, especially for locals. Sometimes, people living nearby don't even realize your business is there until they see it online in search maps.

Communicating is vital. You can use various modes of communication such as e-mail, text messages, phone calls, social media posts, or even traditional mail—choose the methods your customers prefer most. Physical mail is vital if your local customers aren't online much or are scattered across multiple channels. Sending them all a flyer in the mailbox is more likely to be seen by people closest to your business.

Inform everyone about your improved online presence and how it will enhance their interaction with your business. Informing customers could be as simple as saying: "We're now on Google Maps! It's easier than ever to find us and get directions. Check out our website for the link."

It's also essential to ensure that anyone associated with your business—employees, suppliers, or anyone who might interact with your customers—knows these updates. Equip everyone involved with your business with a walk-through of the changes to answer any questions from customers or prospects. This step helps create a consistent experience for your customers, whether they interact with you online or in person.

Step 3: Involve Your Team

Having your team actively shape your online presence is essential to building a consistent and robust business personality. Team involvement could mean engagement in any or all the activities outlined in Step 1. Including your team tasked with updating, writing, or sourcing information or articles for your website, social media pages, or location mapping is vital. Whether it's a staff member, a relative, a freelancer, or even yourself, adherence to your business personality style guide is critical. Unwavering consistency in following the style guide helps build your business's trustworthiness online.

Remember, completing the tasks highlighted in Step 1 forms the cornerstone of your success. While you or your team might be brimming with innovative suggestions or ideas for your online presence, it's crucial to establish a company foundation to build from. For instance, if a team member proposes diving into video content on YouTube before your website is launched, it's your responsibility as a business owner to prioritize what's essential for the business initially. Fun and popular platforms such as YouTube or TikTok might be tempting. Still, your decision should always be rooted in what's best for your business.

Step 4: Provide Resources and Training

In today's digital age, having a robust online presence is a must for your business. Luckily, several tools can help you create and maintain an appealing and up-to-date online identity. Tools such as Canva, a design platform, can help you create eye-catching graphics and logos. Website builders such as Wix and WordPress let you easily set up your website or blog. And marketplaces such as Fiverr can connect you with professionals who can help with logo and website design tasks.

But remember, staying in control of your online presence is crucial. Be wary of services that don't allow updates or changes to your website or social media posts by you or your team. When you can't manage your content, it's easy for your online identity to become outdated. Plus, it can end up costing you more in the long run.

If you choose to handle or delegate your online presence to your team, ensure that you have a clear plan. You should know what, how, and when it needs doing. And don't forget about training. Ensure that you or your team members know how to use your tools and resources. This way, you can keep your online identity current and appealing to your customers, allowing you to deliver on your business personality promise effectively.

Step 5: Refine and Adjust as Necessary

Building an online presence is just the first step toward growing your business. But as we know, running a business isn't a "set it and forget it" sort of thing. It's essential to keep an eye on customer feedback. Are your customers finding any information confusing? Have they noticed anything missing or outdated on your website or social media pages? Take this feedback seriously. Remember, it's your customers who are using your online platforms. Their experience should be smooth and enjoyable.

Don't be afraid to refine your online presence based on this feedback. If something is not clear, make it more straightforward. If information is missing, add it. And if something is no longer relevant or accurate, take it down or replace it. But remember, every change should still align with your business personality style guide. This guide is like your north star—it helps you maintain consistency and stay true to your customer promise.

Now, a system for making these changes is also essential. Maybe it's just you who does the work, or you have others helping manage your online presence. Either way, create a straightforward process. Decide when and how you or your team or contractor should make changes and how you will approve them. This process keeps everyone equally informed and ensures that your online presence matches your business personality. For example, proposed changes are e-mailed to you for approval, or you hold a monthly meeting to review and discuss updates. Find a system that works for you and your team.

Step 6: Celebrate and Learn From Failure

Building a consistent business personality online is a process, and it's okay if things don't go perfectly the first time. Like every aspect of your business, there will be successes and failures. It's important to understand that failure isn't a setback but a chance to learn and grow.

If you implement a particular aspect of your business personality online that doesn't match with your customers' expectations as you'd hoped, that's alright. Take it as a learning opportunity. Reflect on why it didn't work. Was the message unclear? Was it not in line with your customer's needs or expectations? Did it not follow your style guide? Use this feedback to adjust and improve.

Remember also to celebrate your successes. If your online presence correctly represents your business personality, and engages your customers, take time to recognize this. Celebrate these wins, no matter how small they seem. They validate your efforts and bring you closer to establishing a solid, recognizable business personality.

Throughout this process, keep reminding yourself of the uniqueness of your business and the value you provide. Be patient, keep learning from each experience, and you'll see your business grow.

Conclusion

We've talked about why your business personality is important and how to build it. But what do you do when things change around you? Our next chapter, "Embracing Change for Growth," will show you how to adapt to new situations without losing what makes your business special. You'll learn how to spot changes early and how to decide what to do next.

CHAPTER 2

Embracing Change for Growth

Chapter 2 of this book is all about embracing change for growth. As a small business owner, you know that change is a constant factor in today's fast-paced business world. To succeed, you must recognize and embrace change and adapt as necessary.

In this comprehensive chapter, I'll guide you through the complexities of managing change by applying proven project management principles, specifically tailored for small businesses. I begin by discussing the significance of a growth mindset in Section 2.1, where you'll learn strategies to overcome resistance to change. Recognizing the right time for change is essential; in Section 2.2, I delve into key indicators such as declining sales or customer feedback to help you make timely decisions.

A concrete case study in Section 2.3 offers valuable insights by showcasing a small service firm—a hair salon—that successfully navigated market changes. This case will enlighten you about the real-world challenges faced, the strategies employed to tackle them, and the successful outcomes achieved.

Wrapping up the chapter, in Section 2.4, I summarize the key takeaways and provide actionable steps to implement what you've gleaned from this chapter in your own business ventures.

Also included are four project briefs—each designed to give you hands-on tools for navigating change. These briefs cover everything from recognizing and embracing change to developing customer experience and growth mindset strategies.

By the conclusion of this chapter, you'll be armed with valuable insights, practical advice, and tangible tools to confidently adapt to change and improve your business performance.

2.1 Recognizing and Embracing Change

It's crucial to recognize and embrace change to stay relevant. Declining sales or customer feedback due to changes in the business environment are signs that change is necessary. Managing change within your organization on a project basis will make achieving it easier. To effectively manage uncertainty in your business environment and avoid making wrong decisions that lead to poorer performance than your competitors, it's essential to plan well, set clear objectives, and understand the link between uncertainty and company performance.

When starting a project, setting clear goals and objectives is crucial. In embracing change and growth, you must define your dreams, whether adapting to market changes or developing a growth mindset. Having a clear purpose can help you stay focused and increase the likelihood of achieving success.

My research found that small business owners who feel like their business operates in an uncertain environment are likelier to focus on business personality activities. A business personality focus means your company will increase its financial performance because, as we saw in Chapter 1, focusing on business personality increases revenue by up to three times companies that don't focus on business personality.

Start reallocating resources to these activities when changes in your local market are intense, take place continuously, and occur significantly within a year, irrespective of your company's age, size, or level of competition in your local market.

When many changes happen quickly in your local market within a year, it is a good indicator that you should focus on your business personality and improve your services to stay relevant. Small service companies can improve their performance over competitors by reallocating resources to business personality and incremental improvement activities. I recommend that you start reallocating resources to these activities when changes in your local market are intense, take place continuously, and occur significantly within a year, irrespective of your company's age, size, or level of competition in your local market.

Typically, when a company is experiencing an uncertain business environment, with continual or quick changes within their industry, the owner is more likely to focus on managing their business personality if they want to succeed. However, suppose you ignore the changes or pretend they won't influence your business environment because of fear of change or not knowing what to do because the business environment has changed. In that case, you will not take advantage of the opportunity to grow.

Prioritizing business personality from the start is essential because a business's personality is a crucial part of its strategy that creates distinction from competitors, builds customer relationships, and reduces focus on price when choosing a service company. You can ensure consistency in your business personality by developing and implementing a business personality style guide that flows through all marketing activities and materials. In addition, treating the business personality as an asset is crucial as it is the most critical asset of a successful company and can add value when selling the business.

You can recognize changes in your business environment by the intensity and difference of changes occurring from one year to the next. Once you recognize the need to adapt to changing times, it is never too late nor too early to start. Making your business personality visibly consistent across all marketing materials is essential for success. You should also announce service improvements to your local market to inform customers and prospects of your progress.

I encourage you to recognize your business personality as an essential asset, including awareness, reputation, personality, values, imagery, and preferences. Prioritizing business personality and incremental improvement activities are necessary to sustain long-term advantage. In addition, I encourage you to make frequent improvements to your service delivery to adapt to changing consumer preferences and reduce looking like a riskier option than your competitors. By applying the project management principle of setting clear objectives, you can effectively recognize and embrace change, which is essential for growth and success.

2.2 The Right Time to Start

As a small business owner, it's crucial to understand when it's the right time to start adapting to change. Waiting too long or making changes too quickly without proper planning can lead to poor business performance compared to competitors. To avoid this, you can apply the project management principle of breaking down your change and growth project into smaller, manageable tasks. Smaller tasks will help you focus on one at a time and avoid feeling overwhelmed.

In this section, we will explore when the right time is for small service companies to start adapting to change. As discussed earlier, you must understand the signs that indicate a need for change, such as declining sales or customer feedback due to changes in the business environment. But when is the right time to start making changes?

According to my doctoral research, the right time to start adapting to change is when changes in a company's local market are intense, when changes are taking place continuously, and when changes occur significantly within a year, irrespective of the company's age, size, or level of competition in their local market. Applying the project management principle of breaking down your change and growth project into smaller, manageable tasks, you can start by developing a plan that outlines what changes you need to complete and how you will implement them.

Communicating with employees is crucial to involve everyone in the change process and ensure that everyone is working toward the same goals. You should communicate the changes and why they are necessary and provide training and support to employees to help them adjust. You can identify specific manageable tasks for employees and monitor their performance to ensure that their changes are implemented effectively.

You don't have to do it alone when making changes. Seeking advice from experts or consultants can provide valuable insights and help ensure that you make changes effectively. You can identify areas where expert advice is needed and engage with experts accordingly.

It's essential to monitor progress and adjust the plan if necessary. Monitoring can involve measuring sales, customer feedback, and employee performance. You can identify specific metrics to track progress and adjust your plan accordingly.

Change is a constant in business, so it's essential to remain adaptable and prepared for future changes. As a small business owner, you should continue to monitor your local market and adjust as necessary to stay relevant. You can identify specific areas where you need to stay adaptable and plan accordingly.

In summary, the right time to start adapting to change is when changes in your local market are intense, when changes are taking place continuously, and when changes occur significantly within a year, irrespective of your company's age, size, or level of competition in your local market. You can recognize these changes by paying attention to your competitors, talking to your customers, and monitoring social media. To initiate and manage change effectively, you should start with a plan, communicate with employees, seek expert advice, monitor progress, and stay adaptable while breaking down your change and growth project into smaller, manageable tasks to ensure success.

2.3 Success in Action: A Small Service Firm Adapting to Market Changes (Hair Salon)

This section will look closer at a small service company that successfully adapted to market changes. By examining this case study, we can gain valuable insights into the strategy and tactics that you can use to remain relevant and thrive in an ever-changing marketplace.

Background of the company: The small service company we will be examining is a hair salon—that had been operating for five years. A woman who had recently moved her salon to a new location to focus on improving her business started the salon. The owner was passionate about providing excellent colorist hair care design and styling services and building a business she could be proud of that would meet her financial goals.

Recognizing the need for change: After a few years in business, she noticed changes in her local market. There were several hair businesses locally, and while she had a good base of profitable, loyal customers, she wasn't getting as many of them as she had hoped in the new location. So, she realized that she needed to act to be more relevant to find more profitable customers to continue to grow her business.

Adapting to market changes: To adapt to the changes in the local market, she spoke to friends and met with me. We prioritized tasks based on their importance and urgency and reviewed her business and the competition around her business to see the areas that would benefit from improvement. Prioritization helped her focus on the tasks that would most significantly impact achieving her business objectives.

Next, we reviewed her customer base to determine who they were and what their needs were to improve the business environment of the salon to make it more attractive to that type of customer by adapting to the changes in the market that they were getting and wanting from other companies. We prioritized this task because understanding the customer base is crucial to developing a successful marketing strategy. Then, we updated the business personality, creating messages and pictures to make more loyal customers feel they belonged at her salon. By prioritizing this task, the small business owner built a strong business personality that was attractive to her most profitable customers. We then improved the website and social media sites using the business personality and added an online booking to the website. By prioritizing this task, the small business owner was able to diversify service offerings and attract new customers while making it easier for existing customers to book appointments.

Finally, the owner held a makeover party to relaunch the improvements, inviting current and potential customers to view the improved salon and business personality. After the party, the salon owner used targeted business personality messages, customer referrals, and expert haircare tips to promote her salon via Facebook and Instagram, paid and unpaid, to attract new customers.

Results of the company's adaptation: As a result of these changes, the hair salon had an increase of 244 percent in customer leads and was able to grow. She was able to attract new customers and retain existing ones by adapting to the changes in the marketplace, which demonstrated to her most profitable customers that her business could meet their needs better than the competition. She continued to provide exceptional service, something that her existing customers appreciated and offered new services that were complimentary to hair care services. Before the pandemic, that started in 2019, this hair salon was a thriving business.

Key takeaways for small business owners: There are several key takeaways that you can learn from the salon's experience. First, it's crucial to stay aware of changes in the local market and act when necessary. Second, building a strong business personality and messages can help small businesses stand out. Third, understanding who your best customers are makes it easier to find more like them. Finally, using social media can help small businesses reach people outside their immediate circle of family and friends and build awareness and trust with potential customers. By prioritizing these key takeaways, you can adapt to market changes, grow your business, and thrive in an ever-changing marketplace.

2.4 Embracing Change for Growth: Key Insights and Next Steps

Adapting to change is critical for businesses to last into the future. This section discusses strategies for successful adaptation, guided by key project principles.

Earlier sections discussed the importance of adaptability and recognizing signs that signal a need for change. Knowing when and how to adapt is pivotal for staying relevant.

We highlighted a case study in Section 2.3, illustrating successful adaptation through project management principles. The key takeaways are the need for flexibility, understanding the indicators of required change, and efficiently allocating resources.

This chapter features the following project briefs following the Start, Plan, Do, Finish framework:

- 2.5: Recognizing and Embracing Change
- 2.6: Timing Your Changes
- 2.7: Customer Experience Strategy
- 2.8: Cultivating a Growth Mindset

These briefs guide you through recognizing change, timing your adaptations, improving customer experience, and fostering a growth mindset.

In the next section, we'll delve into increasing the visibility of your business personality as a mechanism for attracting new customers. This is a strategic way to adapt to market shifts and strengthen your business personality. Let's get started.

2.5 Start: Recognizing and Embracing Change

Change is a constant in business, and you must recognize and embrace change to stay relevant and succeed in the market. Unfortunately, many small business owners resist change because they are comfortable with what they are doing or fear that change will disrupt their business. As a business owner, you may feel that changing your business identity or personality indicates that you did something wrong, but that isn't the case. What you did in the past worked at that time, and as the business environment changes, you must continue to change along with it.

In this project brief, we explore strategies for recognizing and embracing change and overcoming change resistance. By implementing these strategies, you can adapt to changes in the market, remain relevant, and continue to grow your business.

Objectives

- Help you recognize and embrace change in your business
- Help you understand the need for change, communicate it effectively to your teams, and involve them in the change process
- Help you implement strategies to adapt to changes in the market, remain relevant, and experience business growth

Scope

- Analyzing business performance, customer feedback, and industry trends to recognize the need for change
- Communicating the need for change to your team and addressing resistance to change
- Involving your team in the change process

Deliverables

- A list of strategies for analyzing business performance, customer feedback, and industry trends
- A guide on communicating the need for change to your team and addressing resistance to change

- A guide on involving your team in the change process

Timeline

The project is expected to take approximately two weeks to complete. The timeline will be as follows:

Week 1: Research changes in your market
Week 2: Develop how to communicate the need for change and involve your team in the change process

Resources Required

- Internet access for research
- Access to business performance data, customer feedback, and industry trends
- Access to a team of employees, family members, or contractors who provide various aspects of delivering your service or products

Risks and Challenges

- Resistance to change from team members or people who have an interest in your company
- Difficulty in implementing changes due to limited resources or competing priorities
- Inability to gather accurate or relevant data for analyzing business performance, customer feedback, or industry trends

Key Stakeholders

- Small business owner(s)
- Employees, family members, or contractors who provide various aspects of delivering the service or products
- Customers and clients who provide feedback on the business performance and products or services

- Industry experts or peers who can provide insights into industry trends and best practices

Step 1: Recognize the Need for Change

The first step in embracing change is to recognize the need for it. Start by analyzing your business performance, customer feedback, and industry trends. Next, identify areas where your business is falling behind or your customers request improvements. This analysis will help you recognize the need for change and motivate you to act.

Here are examples of how you could analyze business performance, customer feedback, and industry trends:

Business performance: First, review your financial statements, such as income and balance sheets, to analyze your business performance. Look at trends in your revenue, expenses, and profits over time. Compare your performance to industry benchmarks to identify where you are lagging. Also, conduct a strength-weakness-opportunity-threat (SWOT) analysis to identify internal (strengths, weaknesses) and external factors (opportunity, threats) that could impact your business performance.

In my experience working with micro businesses, I've often heard the concern, "Where can I find industry benchmarks?" While it's true that specific benchmarks for micro businesses might be scarce, it's crucial for you, as a business owner, to keep an eye on the evolving market landscape. If you notice a decline in your customer base, it might be time to review what your competitors are offering. For instance, if they're providing a wider range of payment options such as debit, credit, Apple Pay, PayPal, and more, it could be a sign that customer expectations are shifting. Now, when it comes to conducting a SWOT analysis, I urge you to be brutally honest with yourself. A practical approach is to compare customer reviews between your business and competitors. These reviews can offer invaluable insights into your SWOTs. Remember, recognizing a weakness is the first step to addressing it and turning it into an opportunity for growth.

Customer feedback: Collect customer feedback through surveys, online reviews, or social media. Use this feedback to identify areas where your customers are unhappy or where they would like to see improvements. For example, if you own a restaurant and receive feedback that customers are dissatisfied with the wait times for their food, you may need to change your kitchen processes to improve efficiency. In addition, identify trends in customer feedback over time to see if specific issues are recurring.

Industry trends: Stay current on industry trends through various sources such as industry publications, conferences, or social media groups. As a small business owner, staying informed helps you identify new products or services that may be in demand or changes in consumer behavior that could impact your business. For instance, if you own a clothing store and notice that more customers are shopping online, consider offering an online store or improving or promoting your website to remain visible and relevant.

Step 2: Communicate

Once you recognize the need for change, it's crucial to communicate it to your team. Your team may consist of employees, family members, or contractors who provide various aspects of delivering your service or products. Be transparent, explain why the change is necessary, how it will benefit the business, and listen to feedback. Encourage everyone in your team to share their thoughts and concerns. Sometimes people within the team may resist change because they don't want to lose control of how the business is run or managed. Recognizing why some people may not like the changes will help you be more understanding of other people's resistance. When everyone understands the need for change and is involved in the process, they will be more likely to embrace it.

Here are some general examples of communicating the need for change and responding to resistance.

Communicating the Need for Change

"To stay relevant and attract more customers, we need to make some changes to our product/service to meet customer needs better."

"We've noticed that our sales have been declining, and we need to change things."

"To improve our profit and grow, we must change how we operate."

Responding to Resistance to Change

> "I understand that change can be difficult, but it's important for the business's success. Can you tell me more about your concerns and how we can address them together?"

> "I appreciate your perspective, but we must make these changes to stay relevant. Can we do anything to make the transition easier for you?"

> "I recognize that change can be challenging, but ensuring the business's long-term success is necessary. So how can we work together to make this change successful?"

Here are some specific reasons people might fear change, including you, and how you can respond in each situation:

> Worried about losing their job: Sometimes, when changes happen, people think they might lose their job or get fewer hours. That's like worrying about being unable to pay the bills or take the family out on weekends. So, it's natural for them to be scared. Before initiating such a serious conversation with a team member, it's essential for you, as a business owner, to be well-prepared and clear on a few key points.

> First and foremost, determine the direct impact on their job: Will they still have a position, or is there a risk of them losing it? If there's a chance they can stay on, what would their modified role be? It's also vital to consider the practicalities. If their role is being terminated, will there be a notice period? And if so, how long? Additionally, consider whether you can offer any financial support or severance to assist them during the transition. Plus, if the changes you are making to your business means staff will lose their jobs, help them find a new one. Review their resume, give them a supportive reference, and let other people know you have staff they can now hire.

Starting the conversation is a significant step, but having clear answers and a well-thought-out plan is equally, if not more, important. It not only shows your commitment to your team but also ensures the conversation is constructive and solutions oriented.

> Your response—changed role: As the boss, you can chat with your team and let them know upfront that their jobs are safe. Say something like, "We're making changes to grow, not to let anyone go. You are the engine of this business, and we need you."
>
> Your response—job loss: Say something like, "Hey [Team Member's Name], I wanted to chat with you about some changes we're thinking of making. These might change things up a bit with your job. I really appreciate everything you do here, and I want to make sure you have all the information you need. Let's talk about how we can work through this together."
>
> Your response—job loss: "[Team Member's Name], you know how much your work means to this business. We're looking at making a few tweaks, and it might affect what you do day-to-day. I wanted to give you notice and see how we can figure this out as a team."

Fearing the unknown: Imagine if someone blindfolds you and says they're taking you somewhere but won't say where. You'd be uneasy, right? People in your business might feel the same way about changes they don't understand.

> Your response—fear unknown: Share what's going on. Have a coffee meet-up or a simple team meeting and lay out the plans. Say, "We're trying this [new thing]. Here's what [it is], here's [why we're doing it], and here's [how it could help us]."

Not wanting extra work: Sometimes, when there are changes, it means learning new skills or doing things differently. Some people might worry about having to work extra hard or longer hours.

> Your response—extra work: Explain how the change can eventually make things easier. For example, "We're switching to this new software. It'll be tough initially but save us time and hassle."

Feeling like they don't matter: Imagine if your family decides to repaint the living room, but no one asks for your opinion on the color. You may feel a bit left out for not being included, even if you don't like the chosen color. Employees might feel the same if you make changes without their prior knowledge.

Your response—don't matter: Maybe say, "I've been considering trying a new supplier for [x] to lower our costs. Can you think of any concerns or issues our customers might have with this change?"

Worried they can't keep up: Think of when smartphones first came out. Some people were excited, while others were like, "How do I even use this thing?" Some of your team might worry they don't have the skills for the new changes.

Your response—keep up: Offer training and support. Say, "I know this new system might be a bit tricky at first, but we'll have training sessions, and I'm always here if you need help."

Your concern about perception: As an owner, you might be concerned that by implementing changes, it could appear as if previous decisions were wrong, which could weigh on your mind.

> Change is a natural part of business growth, not a reflection of past mistakes.

Your self-response—perception: Acknowledge that change is a natural part of business growth, not a reflection of past mistakes.

The external business environment changes continually, even if you aren't changing internally. Being able to recognize opportunities for improvement and make necessary changes is a clear sign of smart ideas and good leadership. Share your vision with your team and engage them in the process.

Your response—external changes: "We're making some changes to stay ahead and keep our business fresh and relevant. Change is how great businesses thrive, by adapting and evolving." This approach communicates that the changes are strategic and forward-thinking, highlighting your leadership in steering the business in the right direction.

Fear of losing control: Sometimes, when changes roll in, people worry that they won't be the go-to person anymore or that their say in things will get smaller. It's like being the captain of a ship, and suddenly someone says you've got to share the wheel. That can be unsettling, even though it is necessary.

Your response—lose control: As the owner, it's essential to recognize this fear and address it head-on. Communicate each person's value to the team and clarify how their roles contribute to the bigger picture. For example, you might say, "We're making some changes, but your knowledge and expertise are invaluable. Your role will be just as crucial, maybe even more, as we move forward. You might even find that you can focus more on what you're good at."

It's essential to listen to and address your and your team's concerns and involve them in the change process as much as possible. Also, understanding and fixing the main reasons people don't want to change, like fearing losing control or not knowing what's coming next, can help make everyone more comfortable and supported.

Step 3: Involve Your Team

To overcome resistance to change, involve your team in the change process. Ask your team for input and ideas and give them ownership over the changes. This involvement will give your team a sense of control and being included in the changes, making them more likely to support and follow them.

Here are some examples of how you can involve team members in the change process without compromising your business personality identity or the changes you need to make:

Hold team meetings: Schedule team meetings to discuss the changes that need to be made and involve your team members in decision making. Encourage your team to talk about what worries them about the changes and listen to understand their concerns. You can use this feedback to inform your decision-making process.

Response to resistance: "Thank you for your input; I will consider it. However, at this point, we need to focus on the changes that align with our business personality identity and that we believe will benefit the business the most."

Delegate tasks: Assign specific tasks related to the change process to team members. Delegating will help team members feel more included in the changes and take ownership of the process.

Response to resistance: "I appreciate your willingness to take ownership of this task. However, we must ensure that the changes align with

our business personality identity and are in the business's best interest. Let's work together to find a solution that achieves these goals."

Provide training: Offer training or workshops to team members to help
them develop new skills and adapt to the changes. Training will help
them feel more confident and included during the change process.

Response to resistance: "I understand that change can be difficult, but
offering training or workshops will help us adapt to the changes
more smoothly. Let's work together to find a solution that supports
everyone's growth and development."

Remember, respecting your team members' input and concerns is
essential. But ultimately, as a business owner, you must make decisions
that align with your business personality identity and are in the business's
best interest.

Step 4: Provide Resources and Training

Change is challenging; your team may need additional resources and
training to succeed. Provide your team with the resources to learn new
skills and adapt to the changes. Resources could include training sessions,
online resources, or mentoring programs. When your team feels confident and prepared, they will more likely embrace change.

Here are some examples of training resources that you can provide
your team to help them succeed in improving the business through incremental change:

Online courses: Online courses are available on platforms such as
Udemy, Coursera, YouTube, and LinkedIn Learning. You can identify relevant courses for your team members to take to improve
their marketing, customer experience, and project management
skills and knowledge.

Conferences and workshops: Attending conferences and seminars can
provide you and your team with hands-on training and networking
opportunities. You can identify relevant events in your industry and
send team members to attend.

Mentoring and coaching: Mentoring and coaching can provide you
and your team with personalized training and guidance to improve

skills and knowledge. You can identify experienced professionals in your network who can mentor or coach you or your team members.

Industry associations and trade groups: Joining industry associations and trade groups can provide you and your team with access to resources, training, and networking opportunities. Encourage your team to join relevant associations and groups and cover the cost of their membership if it will help grow your business.

Podcasts and webinars: Podcasts and webinars are convenient for you and your team to access training and learn new skills. You can identify relevant podcasts and webinars and share them with your team members.

Step 5: Celebrate Success and Learn From Failure

Finally, celebrate success and learn from failure. Recognize and reward your team's efforts and communicate the positive impact of the changes. When things don't go as planned, take the time to analyze what went wrong and how to improve. This approach will help your team learn and grow from their experiences, making them more comfortable with change in the future.

An example of a strategy for overcoming resistance to change for a restaurant:

In the restaurant industry, change can be challenging, especially if it involves menu or operational changes. To overcome resistance to change, involve your staff by asking for their feedback and ideas for improvement based on customer exchanges. Consider offering incentives for trying new menu items or training programs for new operational procedures. Celebrate successes with staff parties or team-building events.

2.6 Plan: Determining the Right Time to Start

It's crucial to keep an eye on the business environment and determine when it's time for you to make changes to stay relevant. Here's a project brief to help you plan for change:

Objectives

- Identify signs of change in your business environment
- Analyze how changes in the business environment impact your business

- Identify opportunities for your business that arise from changes in the business environment
- Develop a plan of action to implement changes in your business
- Monitor the results of changes and adjust if necessary

Scope

- Research changes in your business environment
- Analyze how changes in your business environment impact your business
- Brainstorm with your team to identify opportunities for your business
- Develop a plan of action to implement changes in your business
- Communicate the changes with your team, customers, and other stakeholders
- Implement the changes and monitor the results

Deliverables

- A report on changes in the business environment and how they impact your business
- A list of opportunities for your business
- A plan of action to implement changes in your business
- Communication materials to share changes with your team, customers, and other stakeholders
- A report on the effectiveness of the changes and any necessary adjustments

Timeline

- Research and analysis: One week
- Brainstorming and opportunity identification: One week
- Plan development: Two weeks
- Communication planning and materials development: One week
- Implementation and monitoring: Ongoing

Resources Required

- Access to free online tools to search trends
- A team to brainstorm and implement changes—employees or contractors
- Free online project management tools or project book to keep track of progress
- Free online analytics tools to track performance

Risks and Challenges

- Difficulty identifying changes in the business environment
- Limited resources to implement changes
- Resistance to change from team members or customers
- Difficulty evaluating the effectiveness of changes

Key Stakeholders

- Business owner
- Team members—or contractors
- Customers
- Suppliers
- Industry associations or groups

Step 1: Recognize the Change in Your Business Environment

Research to identify signs of change in your business environment and analyze how they impact your business. Then look for the opportunities you can take advantage of because of the changes. Use free online tools such as trend reports, industry publications, government reports, or even some of your competitors to gather data and insights. Remember not to copy your competitors; only follow them to see what they are doing so you can see how your business is different.

Here are some common signs that your business environment has or is changing for a retail business:

- Decreased foot traffic or sales in physical stores due to increased online shopping

- Changes in consumer behavior and preferences, such as alternative solutions to meet their needs, increased interest in different types of materials, products, services, and shops

Step 2: Communicate

Once you recognize the need for change, it's crucial to communicate it to your team. Your team may consist of employees, family members, or contractors who provide various aspects of delivering your service or products. Be transparent and explain why the change is necessary and how it will benefit the business. Encourage everyone to state their concerns about the impact of the changes and listen attentively.

Sometimes people within the team may resist change because they don't want to lose control of how the business is run or managed. Recognizing why some people may not like the changes will help you be more understanding of other people's resistance. When everyone understands the need for change and is involved in the process, they will be more likely to embrace it.

Here are some examples of communicating the need for change and responding to resistance.

Communicating the Need for Change

"We need to update our product/service to better match what our customers want."

"We've noticed that our sales have been declining, and we need to change things."

"To become more profitable and grow, we must change how we operate."

Responding to Resistance to Change

- I understand that change can be difficult, but it's essential for the business's success. Can you tell me more about your concerns and how we can address them together?
- I understand what you're saying, but we need these changes to stay current with what customers want. How can we help you with them?

- I recognize that change can be challenging, but ensuring the business's long-term success is necessary. So how can we work together to make this change successful?

It's essential to listen to and address the concerns of your team members and involve them in the change process as much as possible. Understanding and fixing the main reasons people resist change, such as fearing the unknown, can help them feel better and support the change.

Communicate the changes and their reasons with your team, customers, and other stakeholders. Be transparent and clear in your communication and be open to feedback.

Step 3: Involve Your Team

Getting your team on board with changes is key to smooth transitions. By seeking their input and getting them involved, you build their commitment. Here's how to include your team without diluting your business personality:

Team meetings: Schedule discussions to talk about the needed changes and involve your team in decision making. Use these sessions to address concerns and explore opportunities. For small groups, try these brainstorming techniques:
- Round robin: Everyone shares ideas in turns, no judgment
- Mind mapping: Sketch out a diagram linking related ideas
- Role storming: Team members adopt roles such as customer or supplier to generate fresh insights

If met with resistance, say, "Thanks for your input. Right now, we're focusing on changes that align with our business identity."

Task delegation: Assign change-related tasks to team members. If resistance occurs, say, "Let's work together to find a solution that aligns with our business goals."

Your team has valuable customer insights that can drive business growth. Encourage open dialogue in meetings and directly ask for their thoughts. Acknowledge their input with a simple "thank you."

Empower your team to understand and serve customers, while keeping your business values in focus. Set clear boundaries about who makes the final decisions but assure them their contributions are considered.

Example: A tech repair shop expanding services could say, "I'm forming a team to specialize in new gadgets. You'll document common issues, and based on your findings, I'll decide on the new services."

Your decisions should align with your business identity and best interests. Establish a communication channel for idea sharing but emphasize that suggestions should enhance customer experience and align with your business not personal values.

Guide your team to think customer-first. Set criteria for new ideas to ensure that they align with your business values. If an idea doesn't fit, provide constructive feedback, and direct them toward ideas that reinforce your business foundation.

Step 4: Provide Resources and Training

You and your team need to focus on your core strengths while remaining adaptable to change. Instead of learning everything, I suggest honing skills that facilitate adapting to change and making strategic decisions, including knowing when to outsource tasks outside your team's expertise. First, you and your team should engage in problem-solving and critical-thinking training. Don't try to become an expert in every domain, but rather develop the ability to assess situations, think critically, and devise solutions or strategies. This training will help you to identify what core aspects of the business need strengthening internally and what you can outsource. As you adapt to the changing business environment, you'll be better positioned to make manageable, informed decisions.

Look for opportunities that arise from the changes in the business environment, such as new markets or services you can offer. Shifts in the market can provide opportunities such as diversification, innovation, partnerships, optimizing costs, and focusing on the customer more.

For example, with diversification you could expand product or service offerings to attract new customers, like a bakery that starts offering gluten-free or vegan options to attract customers with dietary restrictions. For innovation, you can improve existing products, service, or the customer experience making your business more attractive or cost-effective, like a fashion boutique creates a new physical store environment that people prefer to shop in than online.

For partnership, joining up with complementary businesses to offer bundled services or products reaches more new customers for each of you, like a food truck that joins with a local brewery to host a food and drink festival. For cost optimization, identifying where you can cut costs or renegotiate with suppliers without reducing the customer experience, like a bakery that switches to energy-efficient appliances to reduce utility costs.

And customer focus, improving the overall customer experience, perception, and repeat customers, like a fitness studio that offers free fitness consultations and workout plans to new customers to understand their needs and goals better.

Consider enrolling in change management training to grasp change dynamics and coping strategies. This equips you to lead during change and helps employees understand their roles. Managing diverse employee expectations is a common hurdle, but you're not alone.

Set expectations: Be upfront about roles and adaptability requirements from the hiring stage. Keep communication open and clarify what you expect, particularly during change. Acknowledge emotions but steer focus toward solutions.

Promote external mentorship: Your time is limited, so encourage employees to find mentors outside the company. This can offer tailored guidance and support. Point your team to local networks or platforms such as LinkedIn, and mention programs such as SCORE in the United States or Help to Grow in the United Kingdom.

By emphasizing clear expectations and external mentorship, you foster a supportive environment without overextending yourself. It empowers employees to find resources for growth and adaptability.

In summary, developing problem-solving and critical-thinking skills, understanding change management, and tailoring your approach to cater to the strengths and preferences of different generations within your team, will create a responsive business structure. This adaptability helps navigate changes without stretching your or your team's capabilities beyond core competencies.

Step 5: Refine and Adjust as Necessary

Implement the changes and monitor the results. Evaluate the effectiveness of the changes and adjust if necessary. Following is an example of what to watch depending on the changes you are making in response to the changes you see in your market.

> Sales: Track your sales data over time to see if your changes increase revenue. You can use that platform's sales tracking tools if you have an online store or a point-of-sale system if you have a physical store.

In the retail industry, you can define a significant change in sales as a 10 percent increase in revenue compared to the same period of the previous year.

Please note that the abovementioned threshold is an example. You should tailor it to your industry, business context, and specific goals. It's crucial to analyze your own historical data, industry benchmarks, and organizational objectives to establish relevant and meaningful thresholds for evaluating the effectiveness of your changes.

Change is a constant in business, and adapting and staying relevant is crucial.

Change is a constant in business, and adapting and staying relevant is crucial. By following these steps, you can determine the right time to start and take action to improve your business.

Step 6: Celebrate Success and Learn From Failure

Recognizing and appreciating achievements and milestones reached by implementing changes is essential. Doing so can increase morale, motivate your team, and reinforce the importance of their hard work and dedication.

One way to acknowledge the efforts of individuals and teams involved is through public recognition. For example, you can announce the successful completion of a change initiative during a team meeting or companywide (family included) gathering. Highlight the specific contributions of team members and express your gratitude for their efforts, and the support of their partners' spouses, children, or parents. By publicly acknowledging their achievements, you show you value them and are proud of their accomplishments.

> Employee spotlight on social media: With the consent of your employees, highlight their achievements and contributions through an employee spotlight on your company's social media platforms. You can create a dedicated post featuring the individual or team member, along with a description of their accomplishments and positive impact. By showcasing their success to a broader group of people, you celebrate their achievements and enhance their professional reputation.
>
> Employee appreciation posts: Regularly share appreciation posts on your social media channels, recognizing your team members' hard work and dedication. You can recognize them individually or as a group, acknowledging their collective efforts in implementing changes and driving success. Include personalized messages of gratitude and tag the employees or team members involved, giving them public recognition, and allowing others to join in celebrating their contributions.

Remember, when utilizing social media for employee recognition, always obtain the individuals' approval. Some employees may prefer not to be highlighted on public platforms, so respecting their preferences and privacy is crucial. By incorporating social media into your recognition efforts, you can use the strength of online networks to celebrate employee or team member achievements, increase morale, and create a positive buzz about your business.

Another way to celebrate success is through rewards and incentives. Consider implementing a recognition program where team members receive tangible rewards or incentives for their outstanding contributions to the change initiatives. For instance, you can offer gift cards, bonuses, or extra paid time off to show appreciation. This approach recognizes their hard work and provides a positive motivation for continued engagement in future change efforts.

After celebrating success, conducting a postimplementation review is crucial to reflect on the experience and identify lessons learned. This review allows you to evaluate successes and failures, gaining valuable insights for future projects. For example, you can gather feedback from team members involved in the change initiatives through surveys, focus groups, or one-on-one discussions. Identify what went well, what you could have improved, and any unexpected challenges or opportunities that arose during the process.

The insights gained from these reviews should inform future decision making and projects. For instance, if you discovered that effective communication played a critical role in the success of a particular change initiative, you can prioritize enhancing communication strategies in the future. Likewise, if you encountered challenges related to resource allocation, you can better plan and allocate resources for upcoming projects based on lessons learned.

By following these steps, including public recognition and rewards, conducting postimplementation reviews, and applying lessons learned, you can effectively navigate changes in your business environment, engage your team, allocate resources appropriately, and continuously improve your change management process. Celebrating success and learning from failure is integral to creating a culture of growth and adaptability within your micro business.

2.7 Do: Develop a Customer Experience Strategy

Customer experience is an essential aspect of any small business. Developing a customer experience strategy that matches your business personality's values helps you provide relevant services and increase customer's coming back, spending more money, and telling their friends and family about your business.

In this brief, we explore this project that shows you how to create a customer experience strategy, including what you need to know, where to find it, how to measure it, and how to make improvements to create loyal customers.

Objectives

- To define profitable customers and create a customer experience that matches their needs
- To map out how and where a customer interacts with a company to find what can be improved
- To identify negative interaction points—what's not working that can be improved
- To implement changes and measure success
- To provide clear guidelines for handling customer inquiries and complaints
- To empower the customer experience team to make decisions that align with the business values
- To train the customer experience team on communication skills
- To set a good example for the customer experience team to follow

Scope

- To develop a customer experience strategy that matches the business personality's values
- To identify the entire customer journey from start to finish and map out each customer touchpoint with the business
- To identify what's not working for customers trying to use your company to improve the customer experience
- To make changes to improve the customer experience tracking metrics such as customer effort, repeat business, and online reviews

Deliverables

- A customer experience strategy that matches the business personality's values
- A list of interactions a customer has with a company—from search to after-sales and repurchase that don't work for the customers

- Guidelines for handling customer inquiries and complaints
- Training materials for the customer experience team on communication skills

Timeline

- Define profitable customers: One week
- Map out the customer journey: Two weeks
- Identify pain points and areas for improvement: One week
- Implement changes and measure success: Four weeks
- Provide clear guidelines for handling customer inquiries and complaints: One week
- Empower the customer experience team: Ongoing
- Train the customer experience team: Ongoing

Resources Required

- Time and effort from the business owner or manager and anyone who will participate as part of a customer experience team
- Tools for monitoring customer feedback, such as customer polls, surveys, online reviews, and social media monitoring
- Communication training materials and resources for everyone delivering the customer experience

Risks and Challenges

- Resistance to change from owner, manager, employees, family members, or customers
- Limited resources and budget
- Difficulty in identifying and defining profitable customers
- The complexity of the customer journey and pain points

Key Stakeholders

- Business owner or manager
- Everyone whose efforts affect the customer experience
- Customers (indirectly)

Step 1: Recognize the Need to Have a Customer Experience Strategy

Having a customer experience strategy isn't just a nice-to-have; it's essential. You see, when you're running a small operation, every customer counts. You don't have the luxury of losing a few here and there; you need to make sure each one sticks around.

A customer experience strategy helps you do just that. It's like a roadmap for making your customers feel valued, heard, and satisfied every time they interact with your business. This isn't just about offering a great product or service; it's about the whole package—the way you answer phone calls, handle complaints, or even the ease of navigating your website.

When customers have a good experience, they're not just likely to come back; they're likely to tell their friends, leave positive reviews, and maybe even promote your company. In a world where word-of-mouth can make or break a business, especially a small one, that's gold.

So, in summary, a customer experience strategy helps you keep the customers you've worked so hard to get and turns them into your biggest fans. And that can make all the difference for your business.

Step 2: Communicate

Communication is important when you're creating a customer experience strategy. First, you want everyone—your team and your customers—to know what you're planning. When everyone knows the plan, it's easier to make it work. Your team needs to understand why making the customer happy is important, and your customers should know what kind of service they can expect.

Another reason to talk openly is to get feedback. Your customers can tell you what they like and what they don't. They're the ones using your service or product. Your team, who talk to customers every day, can also give you good advice.

When your team is involved in making the plan, they feel like it's their plan too. They're not just doing what they're told; they're helping make things better. This makes them want to do their best.

Being honest and clear also helps build trust. Customers will keep coming back if they feel like you listen to them. Your team will also stay committed if they know their ideas are valued.

So, how do you talk about this? Start by explaining why it's important. For example, tell customers: "When customers have a good experience, they're not just likely to come back; they're likely to tell their friends and leave positive reviews which get us more customers."

For customers, tell them: "By creating a customer experience strategy, you can be sure that every interaction you have with us matches what we promise. Your feedback ensures you receive a consistent and reliable experience every time you need us."

Step 3: Involve Your Team

Involve your team in defining the customer experience and collecting and analyzing customer information so they actively participate in creating and delivering it. Their involvement can include creating the persona, mapping the journey a customer takes with your company, sharing customer experience metrics, and then analyzing the feedback to making improvement suggestions based on customer feedback.

Getting your team to ask customers their opinion of your company, product, or service to improve your customer experience will ensure that they understand what is essential for customers and that when it matches your business personality values, it will be consistently delivered.

Holding regular team meetings focused on customer experience are crucial. These gatherings offer a way for everyone to share insights, discuss what's working, and pinpoint areas that need tweaking. This ensures that team members are aware of how their actions directly impact the customer experience and offers a structured way for making ongoing improvements.

You might also want to introduce a simple reward system to acknowledge team members who excel in delivering the promised customer experience. This not only improves morale but also sets the level for what you expect from everyone.

Step 4: Provide Resources and Training

Creating a customer experience strategy isn't about treating every customer differently; it's about focusing on your most profitable customers and making sure you're delivering what they want, consistently. This strategy can even lead you to discontinue services or products that attract customers who aren't beneficial for your business in the long run. To create a customer experience strategy, you must equip yourselves with the right resources and training. You will need training and resources to help you know who your profitable customers are, how profitable customer groups differ from each other, which channels make sense to communicate with them, and personalize how you communicate or deliver services or products to different profitable groups.

For example, if you run a lawn care service and notice that business clients are more profitable and easier to serve than residential ones, focus your efforts there. Use customer feedback to find out how your profitable customers prefer to be contacted and what information they value. Maybe they prefer a monthly e-mail update rather than weekly. If you find that your most profitable customers value quick, hassle-free service, streamline your processes to deliver on this expectation.

Start by implementing a straightforward tracking system to note repeat purchases and customer interactions. This could be as simple as a spreadsheet or a basic customer relationship management (CRM) software. Train your team on how to use this system effectively to identify profitable customers. You can also learn who your most loyal customers are using The net promoter score (NPS) question is, "How likely are you to recommend our business to a friend or colleague?" The NPS question measures the customer's loyalty and likelihood of referring others to your business. Another good way to learn about who your profitable customers are is to ask the ease of a customer's experience with your business. An example of a customer effort score (CES) question is, "How easy was it to find the product/service you were looking for?"

Define your profitable customers by creating a visual picture of what they look like and value in your services or products. For example, a local restaurant might identify its profitable customers as families with young children looking for a casual dining experience. Once you know your profitable customers, you can develop your customer experience strategy based on what is important to them. Once you know what they value about your business, you can deliver it more consistently and focus your efforts on delivering that experience, fixing any issues in the experience you learn by asking profitable customers about their experience preferences with your business.

For businesses serving other businesses (B2B), HubSpot provides resources to build a buyer persona—to identify why profitable customers choose your services to help you target to find more of them. For companies serving consumers directly (B2C), tools such as Xtensio or MakeMyPersona can help you quickly and efficiently create customer—personas instead of solely on surveys. These tools guide you in visually organizing customer preferences and behaviors without requiring extensive surveys.

Next, invest in communication tools that allow you to reach out to your customers in the way they prefer. This could be an e-mail marketing platform for monthly updates, a monthly telephone call, or a text message service for quick alerts. Make sure your team knows how to use these tools to maintain consistent and effective communication.

For understanding customer needs, consider workshops or online courses that focus on customer service and experience. These can provide valuable insights into what customers value and how to deliver it.

Lastly, don't forget about internal resources. Create guides or checklists based on your most profitable customer profiles. These can serve as quick references for your team to ensure that they're meeting the specific needs of these important customer groups and offer additional customer experience training if necessary. Practical communication courses to improve the customer experience are prolific online. Look for ones that cover effective communication, handling customer complaints, building customer loyalty, and managing challenging customer situations.

Training can take various forms, such as group sessions, one-on-one coaching, online training courses or role-playing exercises.

By focusing on these resources and training, you're not just making your customers happy; you're also making the best use of your business resources. This targeted approach ensures that you're putting your efforts where they'll have the most impact, leading to a more profitable and sustainable business.

Step 5: Refine and Adjust as Necessary

Implement changes and track success by monitoring key metrics such as CES, NPS, repeat business, and sales. For example, in a hair salon, you might invest in better chairs or avoid overbooking to reduce wait times.

Actively gather customer feedback through polls, surveys, and online reviews. These insights help you understand customer needs and make meaningful changes. Focus on questions that measure customer effort and willingness to recommend your business.

Regularly monitor and respond to online reviews, both positive and negative, to show you value customer opinions. Choose review platforms popular in your area for maximum relevance.

Social media is also key. Be present on platforms your customers use, not just the ones you prefer. Use social media to engage with customers and address their needs. Tailor your feedback questions to your specific business type.

In summary, customer feedback is essential for ongoing improvement. Aligning customer and business values can enhance loyalty and drive growth. Use the feedback wisely to fine-tune your strategy.

Step 6: Celebrate Success and Learn From Failure

Celebrating successes and acknowledging improvements in customer experience is crucial to motivate and engage your team. It's an opportunity to recognize their efforts and reinforce positive behaviors. Here is an example of how you can celebrate success in customer experience:

> Employee recognition: Highlight exceptional customer service achievements during team meetings or through a recognition program. For instance, you can present a "Customer Champion of the Month" award to an employee who consistently delivers your customer experience. Acknowledge their consistent contributions and publicly appreciate their efforts.

To continuously improve and align the customer experience with your business values, consider the following example:

> Employee feedback and customer insights: Ask your team regularly to tell you about their customer-related experiences, observations, and

suggestions. Encourage them to provide their thoughts based on customer interactions rather than personal opinions. Conduct regular feedback sessions or anonymous surveys to gather valuable information. However, it's important to filter ideas based on whether they fit within your business personality and the preferences of profitable customers rather than catering to a small subset of customers or employees.

Remember, while employee input is valuable, you shouldn't implement all ideas. Consider suggestions based on their fit with your business personality and profitable customer preferences. This fit ensures improvements reflect your business values and contribute to sustainable profitability.

2.8 Finish: Developing a Growth Mindset

Developing a growth mindset is crucial to be prepared for changes that may come your way and to challenge current business practices if they are no longer relevant.

Objectives

- To educate you on the importance of developing a growth mindset
- To provide you with practical steps to challenge current business practices
- To encourage you to embrace failure as a learning opportunity
- To provide you with tools to stay informed about industry trends
- To help you seek out feedback from customers and employees

Scope

- Small business owners who want to improve their business practices
- Covers five steps to challenge current business practices, embrace failure, stay informed about industry trends, and seek out feedback from customers and employees

Deliverables

- Practical steps for you to challenge existing business practices
- Tips for you to embrace failure and use it as a learning opportunity
- Strategies for you to stay informed about industry trends
- Tools for you to seek feedback from customers and employees

Timeline

The timeline for completion will vary based on your needs and your available pace of implementation. Here is an estimate to work from:

Embrace failure as a learning opportunity (two to four weeks)

- Identify areas where you have experienced failure in the past
- Think back on what went wrong and what you can do differently next time
- Implement changes to your business practices to avoid similar failures in the future
- Stay informed about industry trends (ongoing)
- Attend industry conferences and trade shows periodically
- Read trade publications and industry-specific news regularly
- Join relevant professional organizations and stay involved with them

Seek out feedback from customers and employees (two to four weeks)

- Develop a way to get customers' opinions
- Encourage employees to give feedback on their experiences working in the company
- Analyze the feedback received and make improvements based on the results

Set achievable goals and measure progress (one to two weeks)

- Identify specific goals for your business and develop a plan for achieving them

- Decide how you will track progress toward your goals
- Review and adjust your goals as necessary
- Build a culture of learning and growth (ongoing)
- Encourage a growth mindset among employees and colleagues
- Provide opportunities for learning and development
- Foster a culture of continuous improvement and innovation

The estimated timeline for completing this project brief will change based on your resources—time, budget, and people. It is essential to allocate enough time to complete each step thoroughly and to allow for unexpected delays or unforeseen complications during the process.

Resources

- Industry publications, conferences, and professional organizations
- Tools for customer and employee feedback, such as comment cards and follow-up e-mails

Risks and Challenges

- Small business owners may be resistant to change or may not have the resources to implement changes
- Seeking feedback from customers and employees can be challenging if they are not willing to provide it
- Staying informed about industry trends can be time-consuming and may require financial investment

Key Stakeholders

- Small business owners who want to improve their business practices
- Customers and employees who can provide valuable feedback
- Industry publications, conferences, and professional organizations that can provide information on industry trends.

Step 1: Recognize the Need to Embrace a Growth Mindset

As a micro business owner, you likely find that fear of failure holds you back from taking risks essential for growth.

> Plan for success to combat the fear of success or failure.

However, sometimes it's not just the fear of failure but also the fear of success that can be paralyzing. With its increased responsibilities, the thought of managing a larger business can be daunting. Plan for success to combat the fear of success or failure. Create a roadmap for scaling up, including potential challenges and how you'll address them.

Limited resources are a common issue all micro business owners face. Striking a balance between day-to-day operations and growth initiatives is tough. However, even with constrained resources, it's possible to grow.

Think about teaming up with other small businesses that offer different products or services than you. By working together, you both can save money and help each other out.

For example, if you run a small coffee shop, you could partner with a local bakery. They provide the pastries, and you sell them in your shop. This way, you don't have to bake, and they get to sell more of their goods. It's a win–win situation. Or if you provide esthetician services, chat to a local hair salon that doesn't have anyone in-house to share clients. Knowledge shouldn't be a barrier; the Internet is full of courses, and your local chamber of commerce often hosts workshops. Take advantage of these resources.

Resistance to change is universal, especially if you have been doing things a certain way for a long time. But in a constantly evolving market, adaptability is vital. Make it a habit to explore new tools and trends and incorporate them gradually into your business. Don't be afraid to let go of outdated practices.

Networking is vital but exercise caution. It's common for micro business owners to join online and offline communities where everyone is eager to share ideas. While this is beneficial, it's essential to recognize that what works for one business may not necessarily work for yours. The single most common reason for business failure is copying other companies. Sometimes, it can be a case of the uninformed leading the uninformed.

Especially crucial, when seeking advice be very cautious about who you take advice from, particularly regarding business coaches. The Internet, mainly social media communities such as Facebook, LinkedIn, X, and TikTok, is rife with individuals who promote themselves as coaches but have never started, managed, or grown a small business. That's why finding a mentor with experience in starting and growing a company and who can provide tailored advice is invaluable. Ensure that any coaches or mentors you engage with have a proven history relevant to your business needs.

Consider joining mentorship programs such as SCORE, accessible business mentorship and education in the United States, or the Prince's Trust Enterprise Program in the United Kingdom for young entrepreneurs. Another option is MicroMentor, which connects small business owners with business mentors globally.

You join countless successful business owners adopting a growth mindset by navigating your fears, optimizing resources, embracing change, and carefully building a support network with experienced mentors. Be selective, alert, and take steps that match your unique business goals and values.

Step 2: Communicate

Seek out feedback from customers and employees.

Communication with your customers is a prime opportunity to create a growth mindset for your business. Encourage customers to tell you about their experiences with your company. Your employees, too, as they can often have insightful perspectives.

Now, it's critical not to take feedback personally. If you receive negative feedback or something contrary to what you hoped to hear, it's important not to brush it off or become defensive. There could be a gem of truth that could turn things around for your business.

However, it's also good to remember that not all feedback may be genuine or relevant. So, evaluate it critically. But if you start to notice consistent threads in the feedback, that's a sign it's something you need to pay attention to. Genuine feedback is a gift, even if it's hard to accept. It allows you to learn and make improvements that can help your business flourish.

Embrace feedback, analyze it, and use it as a tool for growth. In the long run, this open and responsive approach to feedback can significantly contribute to the success and sustainability of your business.

Here are some specific examples of how you, a small business owner, can seek feedback from customers and employees for a service-based business:

Service-based business (e.g., landscaping, cleaning):

- Send follow-up e-mails after the service asking for feedback
- Have employees ask customers for feedback after the service
- Place a suggestion box at the customer's location
- Ask employees for feedback on the quality of the service and communication with customers

Sample questions to ask:

- How was your experience with our service?
- Was there anything specific that stood out to you (positively or negatively)?
- How can we improve our service or communication with you?
- Did you feel that our service met your needs?

Responding to feedback, especially when it's public, like on social media or review sites, is not just about addressing that one person's concerns; it's a showcase to all potential customers of how you handle feedback. Always respond respectfully, regardless of the nature of the message.

Thank the person for taking the time to leave a comment. If they have shared a concern, acknowledge it, and address it genuinely. Where necessary, offer to rectify the issue. If the feedback is given privately or contains contact details, reach out and engage in a conversation to understand their perspective better. This respectful engagement can often turn a dissatisfied customer into a promoter for your business. Moreover, it shows potential customers that your company has a growth mindset—that you are open to listening, learning, and evolving based on customer feedback. Demonstrating openness to growth through feedback can be a powerful tool in building trust and establishing a favorable business personality—and give you an edge since most small business owners ignore negative feedback online.

Step 3: Involve Your Team

Talk and share ideas regularly: Schedule time to sit down with your team, even if it's family members, and discuss how things are going in the business. Share what's working well and what needs improvement. Be open to everyone's ideas and encourage an honest conversation. Great ideas can come from these discussions.

Encourage continuous learning: Motivate your team and yourself constantly to be learning. Watch educational videos, read articles, or take online courses. Staying informed and picking up new skills can bring innovative approaches to improve the business. Many free resources are available online that can be very beneficial.

Acknowledge efforts and achievements: When someone on your team puts in extra effort or tries something new, acknowledge their hard work and let them know you appreciate it. Even if things don't turn out perfectly, recognizing their effort is essential. It can motivate the team to remain dedicated and look for ways to improve the business. A supportive environment is vital to building a team committed to growth and improvement.

Stay updated on customer preferences and industry trends: Your customers' tastes and preferences might change over time, and it's crucial to stay updated on what they like. Keep an eye on competitors' actions, especially if they offer new solutions or methods your customers might prefer. For instance, if all the other businesses around you are starting to accept debit or credit card payments and you're still cash only, your customers might begin to go elsewhere for convenience. Don't change just for the sake of change, but if you see a new trend or preference that is what your customers want, consider adopting it. If most customers prefer cash, continue to offer this payment term, even if your competitors don't. Show your customers that you're paying attention to their needs and are willing to improve and evolve. It's not always about significant changes;

sometimes, the small things can make a big difference in keeping your customers happy and coming back.

Step 4: Provide Resources and Training

Focus on continuous learning and development. Make education and development a priority in your business. Invest in training programs for yourself and your employees, attend workshops and seminars, and read books and articles on topics relevant to your business. You'll continue to grow and develop as a business owner by staying updated with the latest trends and best practices.

Knowing the latest industry trends and innovations is crucial to remain relevant to your customers over time. Attend industry conferences, read trade publications, and join relevant professional organizations. Knowing the latest developments will help you see new opportunities to achieve your business and personal goals.

Here is a specific example of how a technology business can stay informed about industry trends:

Technology

- Attend technology industry conferences
- Follow industry publications, such as Wired and TechCrunch
- Join the local or national technology association or other relevant professional tech organizations

To develop a growth mindset, being open to change and willing to take risks is essential. By embracing failure, staying informed about industry trends, seeking feedback, experimenting with new marketing strategies, and focusing on continuous learning and development, you will be better equipped to navigate changes in the business environment and grow your business over time.

Step 5: Refine and Adjust as Necessary

Some changes won't work out as planned. When something doesn't work out as planned, think about what went wrong and what you can do differently next time. Here is an industry example of how you might refine and adjust:

> Consulting business: If a new service offering doesn't attract many clients, reflect on why that might be. Did you not communicate the value of the service? Did you not target the right people? Once you've identified the problem, you can adjust your messaging or consider targeting a different group of people.

Remember, embracing failure as a learning opportunity is not about dwelling on mistakes or beating yourself up. Instead, it's about identifying what went wrong so that you can adjust and improve your business in the future. Embrace the process, as frustrating as it might be, as an opportunity for growth and innovation.

Step 6: Celebrate Success and Learn From Failure

When you're working hard to grow your business, don't forget to take a moment to celebrate the wins, no matter how big or small. Maybe you tried a new approach, and it worked, or perhaps you learned something valuable from a mistake. It's essential to recognize that progress and learning are achievements in themselves. Throw a little get-together with your team, even if it's just a few people or family members. You can grab some snacks, play music, and share the successes and the lessons learned. It's also important to pat yourself on the back. Running a business is not easy, especially when looking to improve. So, give yourself credit when you see positive changes or learn something that can help in the future.

Moreover, celebrating successes and openly discussing learning experiences sends your team and customers a powerful message. Your team, whether it's family members or employees, will see your commitment to growth and learning, and this sets a positive example for them to follow. They will likely become more open to new things and develop a growth attitude.

Your customers will also notice your business's improvements and positive atmosphere, making them more loyal and even turning them into business advocates because they'll love what you're doing. Celebrating success and learning is not just about feeling good; it's about creating a culture of continual growth that everyone—from your team to your customers—can be a part of. This way, your effort in embracing a growth mindset is never wasted. It becomes a part of your business's fabric, helping drive long-term success.

Plus, sharing your successes and failures can build a stronger bond between you, your customers, and your suppliers. When you're comfortable doing so, being open about the challenges you've faced and how you've overcome them or the lessons you've learned showcases vulnerability and transparency. This kind of openness is rare but valuable because it builds trust and makes your business appear more authentic.

People generally appreciate honesty and feel more connected to those who aren't afraid to show they're human. The same goes for businesses. By sharing your challenges and ups and downs, you're telling your customers and suppliers that you value them enough to be open with them. Be careful not to share challenges about finding customers, which suggests your company doesn't know enough about basic business practices or potentially can't keep ones because it doesn't deliver its promises.

Trust and authenticity don't just feel good; they can have real business benefits. Customers are more likely to stick with a business they feel connected to, and suppliers might be more willing to extend better terms in times of need or partner with you in unique ways.

So, don't be afraid to let people in. You might be surprised by how much support and goodwill you can get by simply being honest and open about your business challenges to the right people.

Conclusion

We've looked at how to adapt to change to keep your business going strong. But being adaptable isn't the whole story. In the next chapter, "Visibility for Success," we'll talk about how to get your business noticed and make sure people see it the way you want them to. We'll cover simple ways to get the word out and how to handle feedback from customers.

CHAPTER 3

Visibility for Success

Welcome to Chapter 3 of this book, where we will explore practical ways for small companies to make their business personality visible to potential and existing customers. Let's set clear objectives: Our goal is to create a consistent, strong, and well-protected business personality that is attractive to your customers.

In Section 3.1, I will discuss the importance of consistency in building a solid and recognizable business personality for small service companies. Prioritizing consistent messaging across all marketing activities and materials reduces the risk of confusion for potential and existing customers. I'll communicate practical advice on achieving this consistency, which will help you build a sustainable customer–business personality relationship over time.

Moving onto Section 3.2, I'll focus on strategies for protecting and enhancing your business personality, and in Section 3.3, I'll dive into a case study of a small service company's successful business personality visibility strategy. We'll monitor their progress by analyzing their steps, including specific strategies they implemented. Section 3.4 will summarize the key insights and next steps for making your business personality visible.

Sections 3.5 to 3.8 will provide project briefs to develop your business personality visibility strategy, update marketing material, and monitor and respond to customer feedback. Each brief will set a clear objective, break down the steps, and allocate resources.

3.1 Consistency Is Key

Consistency is critical for building a strong and recognizable business personality for small service companies to increase financial performance discussed in Chapter 1. A strong business personality plays a significant role in increasing revenue, more so than incremental innovation.

Let's break it down into building blocks to make consistency less daunting and more actionable.

Identify components of business personality: Before anything else, recognize that your business personality comprises various elements, including awareness, reputation, character, values, imagery, and preferences.

Standardize business personality identity: Creating your unique standard involves using the same tone of voice, images you use, logo, color scheme, and font across all marketing materials, such as signage, business cards, and websites. Help customers recognize your business personality instantly. Develop a style guide as your go-to reference.

Synchronize messaging across channels: Aim for a united front in communication. Ensure that your business personality messaging is the same on social media, e-mail, or print. The tone and language should genuinely reflect the business personality's values and character.

Ensure consistent customer experience: The customer journey reflects your unique personality. From the first inquiry to postpurchase follow-ups, blanket everything a customer can see or hear about your company with your business personality's values and promises.

Monitor and adapt: Watch how your customers respond and be open to making subtle adjustments in response to changing consumer preferences.

Review and update regularly: This is a marathon, not a sprint. You must manage your business personality continuously. Periodically review your business personality components and make updates where needed.

By breaking it down into steps, you can make sure your business's character shows in all your marketing. This helps build trust with customers and keeps them connected to your business, which is important for success.

In summary, consistency is the backbone of building a solid business personality for small service companies. Through these building blocks, you can heighten business personality recognition, strengthen customer loyalty, and secure long-term success. It's about embracing the business personality as an ongoing task and adopting a structured approach to consistency.

3.2 Protecting and Enhancing Your Business Personality

Your business personality is the face of your business. It is the way people identify and connect with your products or services. Therefore, protecting and enhancing your business personality is essential for maintaining its strength and value. Here are some strategies for protecting and improving your business personality:

Trademark registration: A trademark is something unique, such as an icon, symbol, style, word, or phrase, that shows the difference between your products or services from others. Registering your company logo and name with the relevant authorities gives you exclusive rights to use it in your business. Without your permission, no one else can use your business personality or anything similar. Registering your trademark protects your business personality and ensures that it remains distinct and recognizable. Here, allocating resources for legal assistance and the registration process is crucial.

For example, you own a small bakery called "Bake My Day." You can register "Bake My Day" as your trademark, meaning no one else can use that name for their bakery or anything like it. Protecting your business personality ensures that customers can easily recognize your business.

Online presence: Your business must have a professional online presence in today's digital age. Your online presence is anywhere you, your business, owners, managers, and employees can be found online—websites, social sites, and business sites. Regularly monitoring your online presence is essential to ensure that your business personality is presented best. Check for any negative reviews or comments and respond to them promptly. Allocating resources to manage your online presence is essential, and delegating this task to a team member or employing a reputation management service can be incredibly beneficial.

For example, let's say you own a small clothing store called "Fashionista." You have a website and a Facebook page where you post updates about new products and promotions. You notice that someone has left a negative comment on your Facebook page, complaining about the quality of your products. You should respond to the comment promptly, apologize for the customer's experience, and offer a solution to make it right. Show that you care about your customers and are committed to providing the experience you promise.

Enhancing your business personality: Enhancing your business personality means improving its value and perception in the minds of your customers. You can increase customer loyalty and better financial performance. Here are some ways to enhance your business personality:

Consistency: Your business personality should be consistent across your website and social media profiles to your product packaging and in-store displays. Consistency helps to reinforce your business personality identity and makes it easier for customers to recognize and connect with your business. Allocating resources to ensure consistency, whether time, money, or people, is critical.

For example, you own a small coffee shop called "Brewed Awakening." Your logo, color scheme, and signage should be the same across all channels, including your website, social media profiles, and in-store displays. Reinforce your business personality identity, making it easier for customers to recognize and remember your business.

Customer experience: Providing a promised customer experience can help enhance your business personality and customer loyalty. Deliver what you promise to meet your customers' needs and expectations. Allocating resources here to train staff, and delegating authority to them to handle customer issues, can create a committed workforce dedicated to delivering the promised customer experience.

For example, you own a small hair salon called "Trendy Tresses." You should aim to provide a consistent customer experience, from when a customer walks in the door to when they leave. Your consistent experience might include offering refreshments, providing comfortable seating, and ensuring that the customer's stylist is knowledgeable and skilled. A consistent customer experience will enhance your business personality and encourage customer loyalty.

In conclusion, protecting and enhancing your business personality is essential for maintaining its strength and value. Careful allocation of resources and effective delegation are critical elements in this effort. By registering your trademark, monitoring your online presence, investing in consistent business personality, and improving customer experience, you can ensure that your business personality thrives. Trademark registration is a strategic approach and efficient allocation of resources and responsibilities. Whether you are a sole proprietor or have a team, ensuring you address each aspect of protecting and enhancing your business personality competently and consistently, will contribute significantly to the long-term success of your business.

3.3 Success in Action: A Small Service Firm's Successful Business Personality Visibility Strategy (Piano Tuner)

Creating and maintaining a solid business personality is essential for the success of any business, especially for small service companies. This chapter will provide the case study of a small service company's successful business personality visibility strategy. We will explore the steps they took to create and maintain a strong business personality, including specific business personality strategies they implemented, such as creating a business personality style guide and announcing service improvements to their local market. We will also discuss the impact of improving the visibility of a strong business personality on their business performance and the key takeaways for small service companies.

The small service company we will be discussing is a piano tuner. They are a company that specializes in residential and business piano tuning. Over time, they faced tough competition from new tuning companies in their area. However, they created and made a strong business personality visible that helped them stand out from the competition.

Background of the company: The small service company we will examine is a piano tuning company. A man providing exceptional piano tuning and maintenance services for over 35 years started the business. His motto is never to leave a job until the piano is tuned to perfection. Having tuned pianos across the United Kingdom during his career, he wanted to focus on being the preferred tuner in his local area in North Yorkshire.

Having tuned thousands of instruments from top piano manufacturers such as Broadwood, Steinway, Yamaha, Richard Lipp, Bechstein, and Brinsmead, he was skilled with harpsichords, spinets, squares, and fortes. This gave him a clear edge over competitors. However, he had limited experience adapting to changing business trends. Moving from advertising in printed directories to online was a big challenge. This made it hard for the business owner to showcase his expertise in the piano tuning market.

Recognizing the need for change: The owner had a solid group of loyal customers who returned to him for piano tuning every year. However, he wanted to make sure new customers in his local area could find him when they needed an expert tuner. Many competitors in the field were already good at marketing their businesses online, a digital environment he wasn't familiar with. He needed to adapt to stay competitive. Focusing on local customers to replace customers from around England, he decided to talk to people with marketing knowledge. He wanted to learn how to increase the visibility of his business against his competitors. He met me through an introduction by a fellow church member.

Adapting to market changes: To adapt to the changes in the local market, we reviewed his business and the competition around his business to see the areas that would benefit from improvement. The reasons for developing a business personality and making it more visible were identified when reviewing the business to determine what might be stopping customers from using this business. After all, the business provided discerning and exemplary tuning services and an above-standard customer experience. Initially, the company had a Facebook page, a Google My Business page showing basic contact details, and an image of a business card with a piano. Still, there wasn't an evident business personality with pictures and messages that demonstrated the superiority of this company.

An essential aspect of this change was monitoring progress after implementing the new business personality. Keeping an eye on how the new strategy performed allowed the business to make necessary adjustments and measure success. Monitoring involved tracking customer engagement, web traffic, and customer feedback. The piano tuner also set specific milestones to measure the effectiveness of the new strategy in real time.

The process began with a comprehensive analysis of what customers liked and didn't like about the company and looking to see what other tuning companies looked like in the area. This review helped identify how this tuning company was unique and what a natural business personality would be that reflected the business experienced by its current customers and owner. After they created a new business personality and everything about the company was adapted to the unique personality—Google My Business, website, and social media, a launch party increased awareness among current and potential customers, followed by regular, consistent social media posts, paid and unpaid.

Results of the company's adaptation: As a result of these changes, the tuning company had an immediate 20 percent increase in customers, a close to 10 percent increase in revenue year over year, and a 100 percent increase in visitors to their website. Monitoring the progress was crucial for these results. It allowed the owner to see which parts of the new business personality attracted profitable customers. It also showed which areas needed more fine-tuning.

He was able to attract new customers and retain existing ones by adapting to the changes in the marketplace. He demonstrated to his most profitable customers that his business could meet their needs better than the competition. New customers experienced his exemplary service and a better-tuned piano than they had previously with competitors. This business kept growing even when it was closed during the pandemic. They changed their messaging to be relevant and supportive of both business and personal customers during the Covid pandemic. They focused on motivational posts about playing the piano. They also gave tips on how to keep pianos in tune as long as possible until a professional could tune them again.

The impact of a strong business personality on the tuning company's performance was significant. The business personality resulted in a dramatic increase in customers and increased loyalty from existing cli-ents. The company also experienced increased revenue and profitability, achieving financial goals of focusing on a smaller geographical service area. In addition, maintaining the business personality for over four years has increased customer and prospect confidence in the company, with continual new customer tuning requests every week.

This piano-tuning company's success story underlines the importance of adapting to market changes. Plus, the importance of continually mon-itoring progress to ensure that the business personality remains relevant and effective. By setting goals, collecting data, and making informed decisions based on feedback and results, the piano tuner continues fine-tuning its business personality strategies to ensure sustained success.

In conclusion, this case study highlights the importance of recogniz-ing the need for change. Adapting to market shifts and creating a strong business personality are crucial. Rigorously monitoring progress can have a significant effect on business performance.

3.4 Making Your Business Personality Visible: Key Insights and Next Steps

There are several key takeaways that you can learn from the tuning com-pany. First, it's essential to stay aware of changes in the local market, spe-cifically new competitors, and recognize that a company can no longer rely only upon their expertise or the length of time they have been in business to get a steady stream of customers.

Second, it is only through a strong business personality made visible online and offline that a business will be seen and evaluated alongside younger, more technology-literate companies.

Third, it's vital to be open to adopting a new business personality. This personality should reflect the changes in the business environment and competition. This approach ensures that older, more experienced companies aren't left behind. It's not their fault, but the way companies build trust with customers has shifted. Instead of face-to-face interactions or physical directories, trust is now built through digital online methods.

At this stage, it's crucial to emphasize the importance of being adapt-able. Markets are living entities; they breathe, grow, and evolve. So, it's essential to be in tune with this rhythm. Listening to feedback and adapting your strategies can be useful in ensuring your business personality remains healthy. For instance, if the market leans toward a new trend or technology, consider how your business personality can embrace this change while remaining true to its core values. Regularly revisiting your business personality in response to feedback and changes in the market keeps your business current and relevant.

Finally, making a business visible requires a continual, consistent effort to maintain trust with current and prospective customers. Companies that don't understand that their business must be visible and consistent to be considered for trial or purchase will not survive even when they provide the best products or services. Aristotle's suggestion that what isn't in front of us won't be remembered is even more true in the digital age; if your company isn't visible and reinforced regularly, it won't be considered.

> Companies that don't understand that their business must be visible and consistent to be considered for trial or purchase will not survive even when they provide the best products or services.

The case study of the tuning company has shown that a strong and visible business personality can lead to increased customer loyalty, higher perceived value, and new customers, even for older companies.

The next steps for you are to be visible, consistently, with a strong business personality strategy, and always announce service improvements to attract new customers and retain existing ones.

Moving into the next section, we will focus on continuous improvement and innovation. We will explore practical steps for enhancing service delivery and implementing incremental improvement. We will also provide a case study of a small service company's continuous improvement journey.

Practical steps for you to take include the following:

- Announce service improvements to your local market to attract new customers and retain existing ones
- Make regular updates to the business website to remain relevant and current

- Make regular updates to marketing material to stay visible and reliable
- Make regular updates to the physical environment of any retail spaces or offices or store
- Use social media and online business directories to increase visibility in local search results
- Regularly collect, review, respond, and share customer feedback to continuously improve service delivery and adapt strategies as needed

The abovementioned steps improve the visibility of your business and increase your chances of success when many people offer similar services or products regardless of your business's age or size.

3.5 Start: Announcing Service Improvements to Attract and Retain Customers

As a business owner, adapting and evolving is vital to thriving when many people offer similar services or products. Announcing service improvements is essential and key to finding and keeping new, all while strengthening your business personality.

In this brief, we explore a custom way to share service upgrades with limited resources, while keeping your business's true character.

Objectives

To equip you with a cost-effective and streamlined plan for announcing service improvements that match your business personality and build customer relationships.

Scope

- Identifying service improvements achievable with limited resources
- Crafting communications that are consistent with the business's personality and values

- Using available resources and potentially free tools for the implementation
- Collecting customer feedback for continuous improvement

Deliverables

- A simplified plan for announcing service improvements
- A resource-efficient communication strategy
- A feedback collection mechanism
- An evaluation report on the effectiveness of the service improvements

Timeline

- Identifying improvement areas: Week 1
- Developing communication strategies: Week 2
- Announcing service improvements: Week 3
- Collecting and evaluating customer feedback: Weeks 4 to 6
- Generating a report on effectiveness: Week 7

Resources Required

- A small, dedicated team or individual responsible for communications
- Free or low-cost online tools for customer feedback collection (e.g., Google Forms)
- Social media platforms for announcements and customer engagement
- Data analysis tools for evaluating feedback (e.g., Excel)

Risks and Challenges

- Balancing quality improvements with limited resources
- Time constraints due to managing multiple roles in the business
- Potential lack of experience in communication strategies
- Managing customer expectations while implementing improvements

Key Stakeholders

- The business owner
- Any team members or partners involved in the business
- Customers
- Suppliers (if applicable)

Step 1: Recognize the Need to Announce Improvements

> Announcing improvements, no matter how small they seem, can lead to significant financial gains of up to 20 percent.

Starting the process of announcing service improvements is crucial for the success of your business. My research has shown that announcing improvements, no matter how small they seem, can lead to significant financial gains of up to 20 percent through incremental innovation.

Customers need to be informed of your enhancements since expecting them to notice on their own doesn't always work. Many business owners may hesitate to boast about their achievements or think their improvements aren't noteworthy enough, but the reality is different. Customers are naturally inclined to seek out new and improved offerings, driven by their desire for gain and avoidance of risk. By announcing your improvements, you capture their attention and increase engagement and loyalty—buy more, buy more often, recommend to friends and family—opportunities.

Once you recognize the need for this project, you must identify areas where you have or can improve your services to meet your customers' needs. Identifying can consist of any activity you have completed to make how you deliver services or products or the environment you provide them more effortless, efficient, and cost-effective. Take one hour to list five new or improved things in your business over the last six months to share with customers and prospects. If you haven't made changes, pick a few from the following example list:

- Updated website font for more effortless reading
- Added chat communication for customer support
- Added online calendar booking for customer convenience

- Freshened up your store with new paint, lighting, or clean windows
- Spring cleaning for allergy-friendly business space
- Added themed music to enhance your website or store's atmosphere
- Added online booking for customer convenience
- Added more customer testimonials to the website or social media

Step 2: Communicate

Once you have your list of improvements, it is time to let your customers know about them. First, develop a communication plan that outlines where and how your customers seek or prefer information about your company. These channels may include e-mail, social media, print media, or your website.

Use a new tool called "ChatGPT" to help you create messages to communicate the improvements with your customers. If you aren't aware, ChatGPT is an AI language model that enables you to draft content and communicate effectively with your customers.

Here's how to do it:

1. Write a short description of each improvement, stating the benefit to the customer (e.g., "Changed x so customers have y benefit")
2. Create a free account with ChatGPT (see Table 3.1)
3. Copy and paste the appropriate ChatGPT prompts from the following table to craft messages for each communication method, replacing the highlighted text with your improvements. ChatGPT will help you keep your communication simple, direct, and informative. Use plain language and avoid jargon.
4. Share the news with customers over the next two to three weeks using the best communication methods for your business (e-mail, telephone, etc.)
5. After sharing the improvements, measure the impact by monitoring customer engagement, feedback, and sales
6. Create a schedule for regularly updating any latest improvements, product or service launches, or improvements. Because people

Table 3.1 ChatGPT prompt example for communicating improvements with customers

Communication Method	ChatGPT Prompt	Example of a response from ChatGPT of "changing new music selection that matches our business"
E-mail	ChatGPT, help me draft an e-mail to inform customers about our new music selection that matches our business theme. Please keep it under 150 words and focus on the benefits.	Subject: Experience Our New In-Store Music Selection Dear valued customer, We're excited to announce that we have introduced a new music selection in our store that perfectly complements our business theme. This change aims to enhance your shopping experience by creating a more enjoyable atmosphere. We believe that our carefully curated playlist will make your visits even more memorable. We look forward to seeing you soon! Warm regards, [Your Business Name]

are drawn to new and improved experiences sharing your unique improvements keeps your business relevant and sets you apart from competitors.

In my doctoral research, I found that making incremental improvements and announcing them can significantly improve revenue. So, give it a try and watch your business grow.

ChatGPT Prompts

- To use ChatGPT, go to https://openai.com/
- Click Menu
- Click Product
- Click ChatGPT

Step 3: Involve Your Team

Whether you're a solo entrepreneur or have a small team working with you, ensuring everyone involved in your business knows about the service improvements you're introducing is crucial. As a business owner, sharing your vision and objectives can provide a clear direction and inspire the team to work toward a common goal. Discussing the improvements with your team or involving them in decision making can provide fresh perspectives and ideas.

Quick morning briefing: Start the day with a quick chat with your team, even if it's just one or two people. Share the improvements you are making in the business. Ask them to think of any questions customers might have and discuss how to answer them. This way, everyone knows what's happening and can confidently explain the changes to customers.

Team ideas for spreading the word: Ask your team for ideas to tell customers about the improvements. Maybe they have suggestions on the best times to talk to customers or creative ideas for explaining the changes. Asking your team for ideas is helpful because they know the customers well and can help figure out the best way to get them excited about the improvements.

Personalized touch in conversations: Encourage your team to mention the improvements in regular conversations with customers. For example, when ringing up a sale or during a service, they can say how you are making things better in the business. Brief conversations don't take any extra time but add a personalized touch.

Involving your team in this way ensures that everyone is informed with current information to do their job effectively, and it uses their insights and creativity to communicate improvements to the customers.

Also, they can share any feedback they may have received from customers. This two-way communication can help fine-tune the improvements and make them more effective. If you're a solo business owner, consider seeking feedback from trusted mentors, industry peers, or loyal customers who will be genuine and not say what they think you want to hear.

Step 4: Provide Resources and Training

Often introducing service improvements requires learning new skills or upgrading existing ones. Providing resources and training is essential to ensure that everyone can deliver on these improvements effectively. Resources could range from technical tools to improve efficiency to informative materials about the introduced changes.

Training can take various forms based on your business and improvements. For instance, if you're introducing a new digital tool for customer service, a tutorial or demonstration session can be helpful. Regular training ensures the improvements' smooth implementation and increases your team's confidence and competence. For solo entrepreneurs, investing time in learning and mastering new skills or tools can lead to more efficient and effective business operations.

Here are some suggestions on how you can determine what training and resources the team might need to support the service improvements:

Talk to your team: Start by having an open chat with your team members. Ask them what they feel they need to learn or have access to, to make these improvements work. They might have some insights into areas you haven't thought of. Listen to their thoughts and take notes.

Analyze the improvements: Look closely at the service improvements you plan to make. Make a list of the skills and tools that will be essential in implementing these changes. For example, if you are improving your booking system, your team might need training on the new software.

Ask for external advice: Sometimes, getting an outside perspective is good. Talk to other business owners or experts in your industry. They might be able to offer advice on what kind of training and resources are essential for the type of improvements you are making.

Create a learning plan: Once you have all the information, create a plan for training and resources. Your learning plan doesn't have to be complicated. Just outline what you need to get, who needs to learn what, and a schedule for when this will happen. Make sure your team knows the plan and is on board with it.

Follow up: After you do the training and the resources are in place, don't forget to follow up. Ask your team regularly how things are going. They might have feedback or need further training. Being flexible and responsive to your team's needs is critical.

Remember, training and resources are an investment in your business. By ensuring that your team has what they need to bring service improvements to life, you're building a stronger foundation for your business to thrive. The same principles apply to solo entrepreneurs—equipping yourself with the necessary skills and tools will empower you to execute service improvements with finesse.

Step 5: Refine and Adjust as Necessary

Monitor the impact: Monitor the reception of your service improvement announcements and evaluate the feedback received from customers. Monitoring feedback will help you to improve your services and keep your business personality visible continuously.

Customer surveys: After announcing a service improvement, send a short survey to your customers asking about their experience with the new service. Asking customers about their perceptions will give you direct feedback on how the change is received.

Sales data: Track your sales data before and after the service improvement. If you see an uptick in sales or more repeat customers, it's a good sign that the service improvement has a positive impact.

Evaluate the Feedback

Feedback meetings: Gather your team for a meeting to discuss the customer feedback received. Brainstorm what worked well and what didn't. Identify any recurring themes in the feedback that need attention.

Rate the feedback: Create a simple system for rating feedback, such as a scale from 1 to 5. Review the feedback and rate each piece according to its importance and relevance. Focus on the comments with higher ratings, as these areas need the most attention.

Review and update improvement announcements: Regularly review and update your improvement announcements, whether it's every quarter or every six months.

Set a reminder: Schedule a reminder in your calendar to review your service improvement announcements every three months. Use this time to reflect on the effectiveness of past announcements and plan any necessary updates.

Customer preferences: If customers are frequently asking for something or giving specific feedback, make it a point to address this in your next announcement. Show that you listen to your customers and are constantly working to improve.

Ensure business personality consistency: Ensure that your business personality is consistent and up-to-date, each time you announce changes to your business.

Business personality guide: Before making any announcement, refer to your business personality guide. Your guide should have the core values and tone that your business stands for. Make sure your announcement matches your value and style.

Visual and tone consistency: Keep the visuals and tone of your announcements consistent. For example, if your business personality is friendly and approachable, use the warm colors from your style guide and a conversational tone in your announcements.

These steps and examples will ensure that your service improvements are communicated effectively and match your business personality and customer expectations.

Step 6: Celebrate Success and Learn From Failure

Every improvement you introduce, big or small, is a step forward for your business. Celebrating success, regardless of size, creates a positive environment and encourages continued improvement. Celebrating success could be as simple as sharing positive customer feedback or marking milestones in your improvement journey.

Sharing Positive Customer Feedback

Social media shout-out: When you receive a great review or positive feedback, share it with a "thank you" note on your social media platforms. It's a way to acknowledge and appreciate the customer and show others the positive impact of your services.

Highlight in newsletters: Include a chapter in your regular newsletter where you highlight positive customer feedback. Highlighting customer feedback can inspire confidence in other customers and show that you value their opinion.

Marking Milestones

Host a small gathering: When your business reaches a significant milestone, such as a first anniversary or serving the 100th customer, you could host a small gathering or event to celebrate the achievement with your team and loyal customers.

Special offers: Commemorate milestones by offering special promotions to your customers for a limited period. It's a way to celebrate and give back to those who purchased from your business.

However, it's equally important to remember that not all improvements will be successful or yield immediate results. Treat failures as learning opportunities. Analyze what didn't work and why, and use these insights to refine your strategies.

Analyzing Failures and Learning Why They Didn't Work

Conduct a root cause analysis: When something fails, gather your team, and conduct a root cause analysis. It's figuring out what went wrong and why. Getting to the core problem will help you understand the issues that led to the failure, so you don't continue to repeat it.

Feedback loop: If a particular service didn't get a good response, contact customers who experienced it and ask for their feedback. Their insights might shed light on what didn't work from their perspective.

Using Failure Insights to Refine Strategies

Implement changes: Use the insights from your analysis to make necessary changes. For example, if you find out that customers don't like a new feature, consider modifying it or replacing it with something more appealing.

Test and learn approach: Implement changes on a small scale initially and observe the outcomes. This way, you can learn quickly if the new approach works before rolling it out widely.

Celebrating successes and learning from failures creates a world where learning and growing are the norm. Learning and growing is vital for your business's continuous improvement and long-term success. Open communication and being responsive to feedback will show your customers that you're committed to delivering the service you promise.

Whether running your business solo or with a team, adopting a growth mindset that embraces success and failure is vital to continuous improvement and long-term success. Announcing service improvements is an effective way to remain visible to attract new customers and retain existing ones.

Continuously identify areas of improvement and develop communications. Share your improvements and monitor their impact. By scheduling regular announcements about these improvements, you can showcase your business personality. This positions you as open, relevant, and trustworthy. It also shows your commitment to enhancing the customer experience.

3.6 Plan: Regular Updates to the Business Website for Visibility

Your website is the digital face of your business, and its regular upkeep and association with your business personality are vital. It ensures that your company is visible and builds trust and credibility among existing and prospective customers. This project, focusing on regular updates to your business website for visibility, is crucial in maintaining consistency, enhancing search engine optimization (SEO), and reinforcing your business personality online.

In this brief, we explore the process of reviewing, updating, and optimizing your website to reflect your business personality consistently and increase customer notice.

Objectives

This project aims to implement regular updates to the website to ensure a consistent portrayal of the business personality and improve its visibility to attract more customers.

Scope

- Review of the existing website
- Identification and rectification of inconsistencies
- Improvement of website SEO
- Setting up a regular review and update schedule

Deliverables

- A revised and updated website reflecting a consistent business personality
- An SEO-optimized website for improved visibility
- A set schedule for regular website reviews and updates

Timeline

- Website review and identification of inconsistencies: One week
- Website update for consistent business personality: Two weeks
- Website SEO optimization: Two weeks
- Setting up a regular inspection and update schedule: One week

(Note: Time frames are estimated and may vary based on the complexity of the website and the extent of changes required.)

Resources Required

- Access to the website's back end or a website editing tool
- Basic understanding of website management and SEO (there are free online resources and tutorials available)
- Time commitment to review, update, and optimize the website

Risks and Challenges

- Maintaining consistency across all online and offline platforms

- Falling behind SEO best practices
- Adapting the website to changing business needs and customer expectations

Key Stakeholders

- You, the business owner
- Your customers, who interact with the website and form perceptions about your business
- Any third-party providers or consultants involved in website management or SEO (if applicable)

Step 1: Recognize Website Improvements

Review your website: Review your website and identify areas where your business personality messaging and business personality might be inconsistent or different from other places, such as your social media, business directories, or physical retail space. If anything is different, update your website with the same logo, color fonts, and images. Use a similar language style to review and update the words that have received the most customer response. Consistency and repetition are fundamental wherever a customer can learn about your business. Consistency is vital because recurrence gets noticed when many people sell the same type of products or services.

Improve website SEO: SEO is a method to move your company closer to or higher up the first page of local results in search engine results, for example, via Google or Bing. By improving your website's SEO, your website is seen by more potential customers. Make your website more visible on search engine results by using the keywords customers use when searching for your type of product or service, make sure they can view your website as "mobile-friendly"—on their mobile device—and actively update your website. Here is an example of how a restaurant can improve their website's ranking in search results:

Restaurant: A restaurant can improve its SEO by including its menu on its website, adding customer reviews, and having location-specific keywords in its website content.

Set a review and update schedule: Regularly review and update your website, whether it's every quarter or every six months. Ensure that your business personality is consistent across any online and offline places and up-to-date to reflect the current state of your business.

Example for a restaurant: Update your menu, add new food pictures, and include customer reviews on your website.

Step 2: Communicate

Effective communication forms the foundation of any successful project. As a small business owner, you must clearly communicate your intentions and expectations about regular website updates to any parties involved. Parties could be a hired professional, a friend assisting you, or a supportive family member. Ensure that they understand the importance of consistency in showcasing the business personality and how it could enhance your business's visibility. Likewise, keep channels open for reciprocal communication. Feedback, suggestions, and new ideas often lead to better outcomes than planned.

I'd like to stress the importance of clear communication, especially when it comes to website updates, which can significantly impact a business's online presence. Here is an example you can use to communicate intentions and expectations:

Example 1: Kicking off a website update project with a team member or freelancer.

Context: This example is a conversation or e-mail script for communicating the need to initiate regular website updates to a team member or freelancer who will be responsible for the updates.

Script:

Subject: Initiating Regular Website Updates—Your Expertise Needed

Dear [Name],

- I hope you're doing well. I wanted to explain our new initiative—regular website updates. Our website is our online storefront and must stay fresh and relevant. Intention: To keep our website up-to-date, I would like you to take charge of implementing regular updates, including content and design tweaks.

- Expectations: The website should be updated every two weeks. Update the blog chapter, refresh images, and ensure that all the information is current. A simple way to keep our website current is to link to our social media pages—if we post updated information every two weeks. We can use a social media widget to display our posts on our social media pages simultaneously on our website.
- Timeline: I'd like the first update by [specific date].

Please let me know if you have any questions or need anything to do this task. Thank you for your dedication and expertise.

Best regards,

[Your Name]

Step 3: Involve Your Team

Involving your team is essential for encouraging a shared sense of responsibility and commitment. Though you might run a small business with limited staff, any individual assisting you in any capacity can be considered your team. They could be involved in different ways, such as helping you manage and update the website. The idea is to make them feel involved and included in the project's success, fostering a sense of ownership that can often lead to proactive contributions and better results.

Here is an example of involving team members in helping manage and update the website:

Example for suggesting improvements:

Context: You want to ensure that your website remains relevant and is open to suggestions for improvements.

Script:

Hi [Team Member's Name],

As you know, our website is central to our online presence. I believe that continuous improvement is vital to staying ahead.

- Could you please review our website and think about your interactions with customers for any features or elements

you believe could enhance their experience or better
represent our services?

Please don't hesitate to think creatively. I am eager to hear any
innovative ideas you might have based on your interactions
with customers.

Let's talk on [specific date] to discuss your suggestions.

Thanks,

[Your Name]

Step 4: Provide Resources and Training

Equip yourself and your team with the necessary resources and training for
the task. If feasible, information and training might involve familiarizing
yourself with website management and SEO basics through online resources,
tutorials, or even formal courses. Also, consider investing in necessary website management tools or services, like a more advanced website editor or
SEO optimization tools. Remember, the more proficient you and your team
are, the better the results and the less time it will take to accomplish the tasks.

Following are examples of free resources for you or your team reviewing, updating, and optimizing your website to increase visibility.

HubSpot Academy—SEO Training Course (Free)

This course will be beneficial for learning how to improve your website's
visibility on search engines, which is essential for attracting more visitors.
The course covers keyword research, on-page SEO, and link building,
among other topics.

Keywords for further search: SEO basics, keyword research, on-page
SEO, website optimization basics.

Plus, here's an example ChatGPT prompt you can use to learn about
adapting your website to changing business environments.

Example ChatGPT prompt for learning about website improvements
over time:

Hello ChatGPT, as a business owner with a code-free website,
I seek advice on continually adapting and improving my website

in response to changing business environments and customer preferences. Can you provide tips or resources that will help me keep my website up-to-date and relevant?

Utilizing these resources and engaging with tools such as ChatGPT will allow you to maintain and improve your website efficiently without coding skills.

Step 5: Refine and Adjust as Necessary

As with any project, it's essential to have a mechanism in place for regular check-ins and evaluations. Monitor the progress of the website updates and check how well they align with your business personality. Conduct occasional reviews to identify any inconsistencies, and don't hesitate to refine and adjust as necessary.

Here is an example of items for regular check-ups and how often to perform them for one type of micro business to guide you in setting up your tools:

Online Retail Store

Inventory check: Regularly verify that the products displayed on your website are in stock and that product descriptions and images are consistent with your business personality.
How often: Weekly.
Customer feedback review: Regularly review customer feedback to ensure your website's user experience matches your business personality.
How often: Monthly.

Remember to always refer to your business personality guide during these regular check-ups to ensure that all updates and changes align with your business personality. Referring to your guide will help maintain consistency across all website elements. The online world changes fast. For example, a few years ago, most people accessed websites from desktop computers. Now, many use smartphones or tablets. If your website isn't updated to be mobile-friendly, you could be missing out on many visitors. Keeping your site updated ensures that you're reaching everyone and not falling behind.

Step 6: Celebrate Success and Learn From Failure

Finally, acknowledge and celebrate your successes, no matter how small. Each successful website update, and every enhancement in visibility, is a step forward for your business and deserves recognition.

Celebrating success: Celebrating success doesn't need to be lavish.

Team Recognition

Celebrating success can be as simple as recognizing your team's efforts. If, after making website tweaks, you see an increase in views and unique visitors, take a moment to thank your team. Share the latest website visitor statistics, mention how the changes have positively impacted the business, and thank them for their hard work. You can do it through a simple team meeting or a thank-you e-mail.

Social Media Shout-Out

Use your social media platforms to share the good news with your customers. For example, if you've reached a new milestone in website traffic or gained many new customers, create a post thanking customers for choosing your business. Share information with them and maybe even offer a limited-time complementary add-on service to keep the momentum going.

At the same time, don't fear failures or setbacks. Instead, view them as learning opportunities to improve your future efforts.

Addressing Potential Failures

Website Downtime

One of the potential failures when making website tweaks could be unexpected website downtime.

If your website is down, people can't see it or use it. It's like a closed store when customers come to visit. In such cases, staying calm and communicating openly with people who rely on your website is essential. Use social media, e-mail, and text—however you normally communicate with customers, to inform them that you know the issue and are working on resolving it as quickly as possible.

Decrease in Search Engine Rankings

Another failure could be a drop in search engine rankings, which might not always directly result from your actions. Sometimes, search engine algorithms change, impacting how high or low your company listing shows in the search results. In such cases, it's essential not to jump to conclusions and instead analyze what might have caused the drop. Monitor SEO news for any recent updates to search engine algorithms.

Google Analytics helps you assess traffic data and search queries. Based on this analysis, if you find that the algorithm change is the reason behind the drop, work on adapting your website to align with the new algorithms. If it's due to changes you made, work on correcting those issues. It might also be helpful to seek advice from an SEO expert or use free online resources to understand SEO better and stay updated on algorithm changes.

The key is to foster a positive and encouraging environment where you and your team constructively view successes and failures, driving continuous learning and improvement.

3.7 Do: Marketing Material Updates

Regular updates to your marketing materials are critical to maintaining business personality's messaging and identity consistency. In an ever-changing business environment, your business personality and message must evolve to remain relevant to customers' changing needs, and your marketing materials must reflect these changes. Staying current is about adapting to change and consistently representing a relevant business personality.

In this brief, we explore how to update your marketing materials effectively and systematically to match your business personality and messaging, as the business environment changes.

Objectives

The objective is to ensure that you frequently review and update your marketing materials, ensuring consistency with your business personality and messaging.

Scope

- Reviewing all marketing materials (brochures, flyers, and business cards)
- Updating these materials to reflect any changes in business personality or messaging
- Setting a review and update schedule
- Ensuring consistency in business personality across all materials

Deliverables

- Updated marketing materials that align with the business personality
- A review and update schedule for marketing materials
- Documentation of changes made and the reason behind these changes

Timeline

- Initial review and update: Two to three weeks
- Setting up a review schedule: One week
- Regular review and update: Every promotion season or quarter or six-month as chosen

Resources Required

- Examples of industry-specific marketing materials for guidance
- Tools or software for editing marketing materials
- Time allocated for the review and update process

Risks and Challenges

- Ensuring consistent representation of business personality across all materials
- Allocating time for regular reviews amidst other business operations
- Resistance to change if materials have been a certain way for an extended period

Key Stakeholders

- Business owner
- Customers (as the recipients of these materials)
- Any suppliers or third parties involved in the production or distribution of these marketing materials

Step 1: Recognize the Need to Update Your Marketing Materials

Your marketing materials, the visual and textual language you use to represent your business, are integral to your business personality. They not only promote your products or services but also project the identity of your business. However, as your company and external business environment evolve, your marketing materials must reflect these changes. The professionalism and consistency of your marketing materials are critical to your image, reputation, and business growth.

Regularly updated marketing materials that align with your business's personality can significantly enhance people's perception of your company. Marketing material indicates your adaptability to change and commitment to delivering consistent experiences. In contrast, inconsistency or outdated images can reduce customers' confidence in your business. So, recognizing the importance of regular "Marketing Material Updates" becomes a key strategy in your business development toolbox, crucial for maintaining a consistent business personality and adapting to your customer's changing needs.

Start by reviewing marketing materials such as brochures, flyers, and business cards. Ensure consistency across all materials and update them to reflect changes to your business personality messaging or business personality. Update materials to include relevant examples for your industry, such as new menu items for restaurants, sales or promotions for retail stores, or new services for health and wellness businesses.

Auto repair shop: Update your business cards and flyers to reflect new services or specials.

Set a Review and Update Schedule

Regularly review and update your marketing materials, whether every time you run a new promotion, month, quarter, or every six months. Set a reasonable schedule to review and update your marketing materials, whether every new promotion season, month, quarter, or every six months. During each review, make sure that your business personality is consistent and up-to-date. You can also use this opportunity to update your materials to reflect changes to your business personality messaging or business personality. By doing so, you can ensure that your marketing materials accurately represent your business and the message you want to communicate to your customers.

However, it's important to remember that consistency is critical regarding your business personality identity. Changing your business personality too often can confuse your current and potential customers and may even cause them to lose trust in your business. It's because they may start to think that you don't know what you're doing, which can lead to a loss of confidence that you will be able to deliver on your business personality promise. Therefore, it's crucial to ensure that any changes you make are necessary and align with your business personality's messaging and values.

Step 2: Communicate

Clear, consistent communication is paramount when updating your marketing materials. You must communicate any changes to your business personality everywhere and however people learn about your business—e-mail, text, social media, or website. Make sure your new messaging is easy to understand.

Talk about benefits and use images that show customer experience: When crafting your messaging, focus on the benefits of your products or services. Explain how your product or service can positively impact the customer's life. Also, use images that show a customer experiencing these benefits. For example, if you are selling ergonomic chairs, include images of a satisfied customer comfortably working at their desk and text highlighting the health and productivity benefits of using the chair.

> Use images that show a customer experiencing these benefits.

Feedback from unbiased professional sources: Seek input from professional sources that do not have a personal relationship with you and thus have no reason to be biased. These could include industry peers, mentors, or professional advisers. Ensure that these sources have no vested interest in being liked by you so that they can provide honest and constructive feedback. Be cautious not to ask friends or family, as their relationship with you may impact the honesty and impartiality of their feedback.

Don't shy away from repeating the message. Repetition can reinforce the message and make it stick. The impact of repeating messages on consumer behavior is significant.

Company recall: Repeating your message can enhance company recall. When customers are exposed to the same message multiple times, they are more likely to remember your company. For example, consistently communicating the ecofriendliness of your products will make customers start associating your company with environmental sustainability.

Building trust with consistency: Customers will likely develop trust in your company when you repeat a message consistently. Consistent messaging signifies reliability and commitment. For instance, if you always communicate about the high quality of your products, consumers are more likely to trust that they are indeed of high quality, unless customers' reviews say otherwise. Like fake news, repeating something untrue doesn't make it fact.

Always remember to communicate the reasons behind these changes to your team. Doing so makes them more likely to understand, support, and correctly implement these changes. Use e-mails, team meetings, and one-on-one discussions to keep everyone informed.

Brief team catch-ups: Given the time constraints of running a micro business, it's essential to communicate effectively without long meetings. Opt for brief catch-ups with your team, perhaps at the start of the day or week, to quickly go through any critical changes in marketing materials. Catch-ups don't need to be a formal meeting but rather a quick chat to ensure that everyone has current information.

Step 3: Involve Your Team

Involve your team in the process of updating marketing materials. Ensure that everyone knows the changes and promote ownership and confidence. If you have a small team or are a sole proprietor, consider getting input from trusted professionals who understand your industry. Be cautious with seeking feedback from friends or family, as they may have a vested interest in your relationship and might not provide unbiased feedback. Use the insights your team has gained through customer interactions to refine your materials, ensuring that your messaging is clear, compelling, and aligned with your company's personality. Involving your team improves the overall result.

Feedback collection: Ask your team members, whether employees or contractors, to briefly note any feedback they have received or overheard from customers regarding your marketing materials. Feedback could include customer comments on what they find appealing, confusing, unattractive, misleading, missed out, or not mentioned.

By involving your team in a streamlined and time-conscious manner, you can ensure that the updated marketing materials reflect your company's personality, are customer-focused, and are based on real insights from those who interact with your customers regularly.

Step 4: Provide Resources and Training

You must give your team what they need to update your marketing materials. If you have limited resources, there are cost-effective options you can use to create professional marketing materials. Here are a few resources you will find helpful:

Snappa: Snappa is an easy-to-use online tool for creating graphics for marketing materials. It has an easy-to-use interface, and the free version has quite generous features.

Vistaprint: If you need to print your marketing materials, Vistaprint is an online printing company with customizable templates for business cards, brochures, banners, and more. Compare with other providers to ensure the best terms for your business.

Moreover, encourage your team to self-learn through these platforms and share any valuable tutorials or guides they find. Not only will their learning help them in their current role with your company but also will help them find new roles. You can ask everyone to send you links to the material they find helpful to share with the rest of the team. This way, you provide resources and create an environment of learning as a standard business practice within your team, which is invaluable for morale.

Step 5: Refine and Adjust as Necessary

Remember that updating your marketing materials is not a one-time process but an ongoing process. As the internal and external environments around your business changes, so should your marketing materials. Perform periodic reviews and adjust as necessary. Updating your marketing materials is an ongoing process. Based on the industry your business is in, the frequency of reviews and adjustments can vary for example:

E-commerce Stores

- Weekly: Monitor website traffic and conversion rates, as online trends can change rapidly
- Monthly: Review customer feedback and queries to see if product information or images need updating
- Quarterly: Evaluate the overall design and layout of the website and ensure that the checkout process remains smooth and efficient

It's also essential to consider customer and team feedback during these reviews. Listen to their perspectives, as they can provide valuable insights that can help fine-tune your marketing materials. Keep an open mind and be ready to make necessary adjustments to improve continually. In terms of customer feedback, look out for:

Ambiguity or confusion: If customers ask many questions, you think are already answered in your marketing materials, it could indicate that the information isn't clear enough or complete.

It's important to notice genuine customer engagement from casual (friends and family or other supportive business owners who aren't customers) social media interactions and not to rely solely on social media metrics to assess the clarity of your marketing material. Remember just because your friends or family like something, doesn't mean customers do. In cases where you usually have high engagement from actual customers, that's when a sudden drop or lack of attention should be cause for concern.

Step 6: Celebrate Success and Learn From Failure

Each step you take toward updating your marketing materials is an achievement that brings you closer to a more consistent and effective business personality. Celebrate these victories, no matter how small.

An Example of a Simple Way to Celebrate Success

Share the good news: Post a thank you message on your social media or company's communication channel, acknowledging the team's hard work and the positive feedback received from customers. Ask customers to share their opinion of your new marketing materials.

At the same time, it's essential to realize that not every update will be a resounding success. The reality is every business owner, and most marketing professionals, have made errors or omissions in marketing materials since the beginning of time. It's normal and not the end of the world.

An Example of Spotting and Addressing Failures

> Feedback analysis: Keep an ear out for feedback from customers. If you notice recurring concerns or criticisms, it's time to reevaluate. Look at the specific things customers highlight and consider modifying to address their issues.

In cases where updates don't have the desired effect, or there are issues, it's always best to let your customers know you're aware of the shortcomings and actively addressing them. It's an opportunity to show that your company is constantly learning and growing and that you're grateful for the opportunity to serve them better. This transparency can build trust and loyalty among your customers.

Remember, each failure is a chance to improve. Adopt a growth mindset, and don't be afraid to make the necessary adjustments. This approach will propel you toward tremendous success in the long run.

3.8 Finish: Monitoring and Responding to Customer Feedback

It's crucial to realize the significance of monitoring and responding to customer feedback in your business. This aspect helps you understand what your business is doing well at and highlights areas of improvement. Your responses to customer feedback send a message to potential customers about your commitment to quality service and customer satisfaction. If left unchecked or not responded, this could negatively impact your business's reputation and profitability.

In this brief, we delve into the critical processes of monitoring and responding to customer feedback to ensure a positive business reputation.

Objectives

The key aim of this project is to establish a way for monitoring and responding to customer feedback to improve your business reputation and ensure a consistent customer experience.

Scope

- Set up an online search system to monitor customer feedback
- Develop a response strategy for dealing with both positive and negative feedback
- Categorize customer feedback into common types
- Implement changes based on feedback, ensuring they align with your profitable customer base

Deliverables

- A system to consistently monitor customer feedback online
- A set of guidelines for responding to different types of customer feedback
- A categorized list of common customer feedback types
- A plan to implement changes based on customer feedback and monitor their impact

Timeline

- Weeks 1 to 2: Set up online feedback monitoring
- Weeks 3 to 4: Develop a feedback response strategy
- Week 5: Categorize common types of customer feedback
- Weeks 6 to 8: Implement changes based on customer feedback
- Week 9 onward: Monitor the impact of changes and make necessary adjustments

Resources Required

- A team member or outsourced service to monitor online feedback
- Access to all customer feedback channels (social media, review sites, and e-mails)

- Team brainstorming sessions to develop response strategies
- Necessary tools or software for categorizing and analyzing feedback
- Time and resources for implementing changes based on feedback

Risks and Challenges

- Inadequate resources for consistent monitoring of feedback
- Failure to effectively respond to negative feedback
- Changes implemented might not align with profitable customer expectations
- Time required to see visible results from changes made

Key Stakeholders

- Business owners: To approve and support the project
- Team members: To be involved in the monitoring and response process
- Customers: Their feedback is the foundation of the project

Step 1: Recognize the Need for Responding to Customer Feedback

Monitoring and responding to customer feedback is one of the most critical components of keeping a business visible to attract profitable customers. Whether positive or negative, customer feedback provides valuable insights into what your business is doing well and where you can improve. More importantly, customer feedback is used by prospective customers when deciding whether to choose your company.

For example, suppose you have reviews online that haven't been responded to. In that case, it gives the impression that either the company is no longer operating, isn't professional, or, at worst, doesn't care what customers think about their business. Whether or how a company responds to customer feedback shows other potential customers how they will be treated if they use that company. Therefore, it is vital to recognize the need for this project and its importance in the business landscape.

Step 2: Communicate

Once the need for the project is recognized, it's time to communicate its importance. You need to articulate to your team and relevant stakeholders how unattended feedback can lead to the misconception that the company no longer operates or doesn't care about its customers' opinions. Highlight how prompt and proper responses to customer feedback can help shape the perception of potential customers and improve the overall customer experience and retention. Here are why your responsiveness matters:

Consider this: A study by ReviewTrackers found that over 50 percent of customers expect a response to their online reviews within a week. More concerning is that a staggering 63.3 percent of respondents said they've never received a response after leaving a review. By responding promptly, you can stand out and show your customers that you genuinely care about their input and are proactive in improving their experience.

Moreover, a Bazaarvoice report highlighted the impact of your responses. When businesses reply to reviews, customers often revise their original posts, improving their star rating by an average of 0.7 stars. That's a substantial difference on a 5-star scale! So, every response you make can directly enhance your public image.

Lastly, let's think about retention. Companies who respond to feedback retain more customers. Those customers, feeling heard and appreciated, are more likely to stay and recommend your business to others. Additionally, not responding can create a perception that you're either no longer in business or don't care about your customers' thoughts.

By focusing on prompt and appropriate responses, you're not just managing feedback; you are shaping the perception of your business's personality, improving customer experience, and increasing your retention rates. Keep these figures in mind as you strive to deliver the experience customer expect from you consistently.

Responding promptly. The definition of "prompt" can vary depending on the specific customer service channel. If you haven't given customers a feedback response time frame, here is one common expectation:

Social media: On platforms such as Twitter or Facebook, a response within 1 to 2 hours is expected, though responding within 30 minutes can significantly enhance customer satisfaction.

Remember that this is a general guideline and customer expectations can vary depending on the urgency of their issue, the channel they're using, and the norms in your industry. Consistently quick and meaningful responses across all channels will contribute to positive customer experiences.

Step 3: Involve Your Team

Involving your team in monitoring and responding to customer feedback is vital. To monitor customer opinion, set up an online search to gain insights into customer experience and identify areas where you can improve. Here are the steps to follow:

a. First, open your web browser (e.g., Google Chrome, Safari, Firefox)
b. Go to www.google.com/alerts
c. In the search bar, type the name of your company or the product you want to get updates for. For example, if you want to get updates about "Joy's Candles," type "Joy's Candles" in the search bar
d. Choose the type of results you want to get alerts for. Select "Everything"
e. Choose how often you wish to receive alerts. You can select "As-it-happens," "Once a day," or "Once a week"
f. Choose the e-mail address you want to receive alerts at
g. Click on the "Create Alert" button

Once you have set up the alert, share the e-mail alerts with your team so they see first-hand what customers are saying. It's also a good reminder for everyone that customers' opinion is what matters most in prioritizing tasks.

Step 4: Provide Resources and Training

Equip your team with the necessary tools, such as Google Alerts, to monitor customer feedback effectively.

Regularly review and respond to feedback to show customers you value their opinion. Furthermore, train your team on how to respond professionally to customer feedback.

It's important to note that business owners' worst mistake is not responding to negative customer feedback publicly or privately. In today's world, customers are free to share their opinions online, and ignoring terrible feedback can cause them to escalate their complaints, damaging the business's reputation and potential closure. On the other hand, responding to customer feedback, good or bad, shows customers how they will be treated if they provide feedback. Therefore, when you ignore negative feedback, you give the impression to potential customers that their negative feedback will also be ignored by your company. Giving the impression that negative customer feedback isn't essential can be detrimental to small businesses, especially with a lot of competition or alternatives.

Therefore, it's crucial to take a respectful approach to customer feedback and respond to it promptly and professionally. Responding to feedback shows customers that you value their opinion. It also allows you to address any issues they may have had and turn a negative experience into a positive one.

Categorize feedback into one of the following five areas:

1. Positive feedback about your product or service
2. Negative feedback about your product or service
3. Feedback about customer experience
4. Feedback about pricing
5. Feedback about the website or online presence

After you have categorized, respond to each type of feedback in a personalized manner. Here is an example of a response to negative feedback:

Negative feedback: Apologize for any inconvenience or issue experienced and offer a solution or compensation to make it right.

Here is an example for a Health and Wellness company:

Complaint: "The gym was overcrowded, and I couldn't use the equipment I wanted." Response: "We apologize for the inconvenience. We're working to address the issue and appreciate your feedback."

Remember, responding to customer feedback is not only important for retaining current customers but also crucial for attracting new ones. The saying "it's cheaper to keep a current customer than it is to find a new one" still holds true. In addition, it shows that you care about your customers to ensure they have a positive customer experience.

Step 5: Refine and Adjust as Necessary

After monitoring, categorizing, and responding to feedback consider implementing changes based on the feedback received. Changes could involve adjusting pricing, improving customer experience, updating website content, or changing the product or service offered. Ensure that the feedback is relevant and aligned with your most profitable customers before changing.

It's crucial to avoid making changes based on one or a few pieces of feedback that aren't aligned with your business personality, as it can alienate your good customers and cause you to lose their trust. After implementing changes, communicate with your customers about what you are doing and why, and monitor the results of your implemented changes. Regularly review and consider the impact of the changes and adjust as needed to deliver the promised customer experience.

Understanding the importance of refining and adjusting based on feedback is one thing, but seeing it in action can provide a template for you to follow. Following is a real-world scenario to illustrate how you might navigate feedback and make changes.

Home-based bakery:

- Feedback: Multiple customers suggest offering gluten-free options as they or their friends have gluten allergies.
- Decision: The baker researches gluten-free recipes and decides to introduce a limited range of gluten-free products. However, they ensure that these products align with the bakery's brand of using organic and high-quality ingredients.
- Communication: The bakery announces the new gluten-free range on their website, social media, and through an e-mail newsletter, explaining the reasons behind the addition.

- Review: After a few weeks, the baker reviews sales data and customer feedback. If the gluten-free range is popular and profitable, they might consider expanding it. If not, they might decide to offer it only on specific days or as a special order.

Step 6: Celebrate Success and Learn From Failure

In managing customer feedback, there will be successes and failures. Responding to customer feedback is not only important for retaining current customers but also crucial for attracting new ones. It shows that you care about your customers and aim to ensure that they have a positive customer experience. Therefore, as you make changes and improvements are realized, it is important to celebrate these successes.

Customer feedback appreciation day: Create an event such as a "Customer Feedback Appreciation Day," acknowledging and celebrating all customers who have taken the time to provide feedback. This event could involve sending out a personalized thank you note and a small gift, such as an item with your logo from your business or a unique keepsake, symbolizing their importance in shaping your business. Also, spotlight some of the changes made due to customer feedback to highlight that their opinion makes a difference.

Internal team recognition: Recognize and reward your team's efforts in managing customer feedback. You could hold an internal event highlighting examples of well-managed customer feedback and positive outcomes. Such recognition motivates the team and emphasizes the importance of handling customer feedback effectively.

However, it's just as important to learn from failures. You should consider setbacks or negative responses as growth learning opportunities to refine your approach.

Common Error in Responding to Customer Feedback

Ignoring or arguing with negative feedback: Some business owners make the mistake of ignoring negative feedback or even arguing with customers publicly. Both approaches can damage the business's reputation. Ignoring feedback gives the impression that the company does not value its customers' opinions, and arguing can escalate the situation and portray the business negatively.

Ways to Fix Common Mistakes in Responding to
Customer Feedback

Acknowledge publicly, address privately: Instead of ignoring or arguing with negative feedback, acknowledge it publicly and address it privately. A public acknowledgment shows other customers that you value their opinions, while privately addressing the issue with the customer demonstrates your commitment to resolving their concerns without airing the details publicly.

Always remember to keep an open mind and be patient, as it may take time for customers to notice and appreciate the changes you have made.

Conclusion

You've learned how to get your business noticed. So, what comes next? The key to staying successful is to keep improving. In Chapter 4, "Continuous Growth and New Ideas," we'll go over how to keep getting better without losing what makes your business unique. We'll discuss small changes that can make a big difference and how to keep track of what's working.

CHAPTER 4

Continuous Growth and New Ideas

Unlocking Your Business Potential

This chapter will discuss the importance of continuous growth and innovation for small service businesses like yours. I'll cover practical steps to enhance your services, embrace incremental improvement, and share a real-life success story of a small business that focuses on continuous improvement. I'll also provide project briefs to help you apply these principles to your business. I aim to provide clear and actionable steps to drive continuous growth and innovation in your business.

Section 4.1 covers the essential role of customer experience in your business, leading to increased loyalty and positive word-of-mouth. I'll discuss the importance of feedback, employee training, and making it easy for customers to share their opinions. Your objective here is to increase the customer retention rate and improve the overall customer effort score through enhanced customer service.

In Section 4.2, I'll discuss the concept of incremental improvement, which involves making small, ongoing changes to your business. I'll explore how to research your market, generate new ideas, and test them before implementation. I'll break down this process into manageable, prioritized steps based on their potential impact on business growth.

Section 4.3, success in action case study, will examine how a small animal care clinic continuously improved its business. I'll outline their steps, offering you insights into their strategy. This case allows you to assess what was effective for them and consider how you can adapt those strategies for your business.

Section 4.4 summarizes the key takeaways from the chapter and guides you on applying continuous improvement and innovation principles to your business. I'll communicate these key takeaways clearly for adapting the steps provided based on your business's unique circumstances.

You'll also find a series of actionable project briefs tailored to the key aspects of your business growth. You'll learn how to effectively use customer feedback to make positive changes, improve your customer experience and understand your market better, gain insights into identifying and meeting profitable customer needs, and prioritize marketing and business personality for rapid growth.

Throughout this chapter, I'll provide practical guidance to help you implement continuous growth and innovation strategies in your small service business.

4.1 Enhancing Your Services for Customer Experience

In this section, I'll discuss about why small business owners like you must keep improving how you serve your customers. Providing a consistent experience is critical to building a good reputation, keeping loyal customers, and, ultimately, ensuring the success of your business. Your objective here is to increase the number of customers who come back to your business again, and again, and improve customer rating scores, through an enhanced customer experience.

Why Great Customer Experience Matters

Making incremental tweaks to how you manage, run, and operate your business impacts the customer's experience with your company, significantly affecting the business's financial performance. Business owners who fear or are resistant to change, believing "if it isn't broke, don't fix it," are unlikely to achieve the financial success their company deserves.

Being open to and embracing incremental tweaks to how you run your business to keep it relevant for customers as the business environment changes are vital to maintaining a sustainable business. My doctoral research indicated that similar to the concept of business personality, business owners and managers who make minor improvements frequently to their services, how they are delivered, and by introducing new services, achieve higher financial performance. This contrasts with competitors who don't implement improvements as they are needed. If you've ever heard of Kaizen, a Japanese term meaning "continuous improvement," it emphasizes the power of incremental positive changes over time. My research suggests that this principle of continuous improvement is just as vital for small businesses as it is for more established ones. In addition, making frequent improvements and sharing news of the progress with customers provide the most significant revenue return on marketing investment or cost.

You need to improve your services continuously.

There are many benefits to incremental improvements. The main one is financial. Incremental improvements account for 17 percent of company performance. Revenue increases as customers keep returning because of continual improvements, which gives them confidence that the company can continue to meet their needs

> Incremental improvements account for 17 percent of company performance.

and preferences as they evolve. People are more likely to buy more, buy more often, and tell others about your business when they are happy. This positive word-of-mouth can lead to increased sales and more customers without you spending extra money. Loyal customers also tend to be more understanding if something goes wrong.

Figure 4.1 shows how making small improvements can affect your company's finances.

As you can see from the figure, the more you do incremental improvements, the higher your revenue will be. This is the same for young or old companies, and the results of improvements are the same.

Older companies are less likely to make incremental improvements over time, leading to their eventual decline. In contrast, newer companies recognize the importance of continuous improvement and appear more innovative. They apply current business trends that weren't accessible to older firms. Additionally, older business owners, being less risk-averse, often resist change, sticking to what worked in the past even if it's no longer relevant. They are also held back simply by the sheer number of changes that have occurred since they started their business, especially with the fast speed of technology change. This means if you aren't familiar with technology, simply because you didn't need to use it for most of your

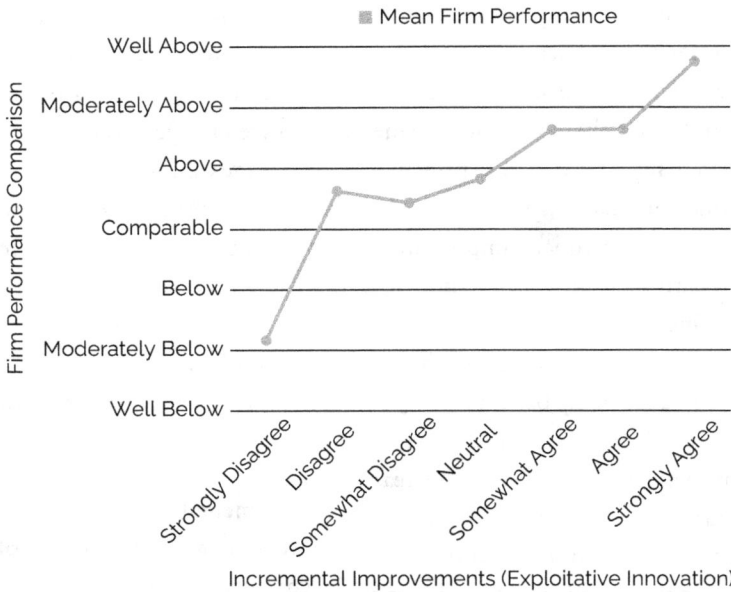

Figure 4.1 Impact of making incremental improvements on financial performance in small service firms

Source: DBA Thesis, Dr. Raewyn Sleeman, 2020.

business life, it makes owners more reluctant to incrementally improve. This reluctance can hinder growth, whereas embracing improvements, getting help from others, if necessary, could enhance their business.

How to Improve Your Services

To prioritize improvements that provide the highest link to financial performance, start by simply announcing any upgrades you are making as you make them. Use your existing website, social media pages, e-mail, telephone, chat, mail, in-person, whatever you are currently using, to share news of all and any improvements you make to improve how your business runs, operates, and provides services or improvements to services. This might sound basic, but it's statistically significant to improve financial performance simply by sharing all improvements to your business.

The words "new" or "improved" can be very important for business owners. These words connect with a basic human interest in finding things that are better or different. When people see something labeled as "new" or "improved," they pay more attention. For you, this can mean more customers looking at your services or products. It's like a signal that says, "This might be better than what you have now." It can make people curious and want to try what you offer. But it's also a sign to be careful and think about if it's better. Using "new" or "improved" in your business can help you get noticed and sell more, but it must be true and match what customers really want.

Second, continue to improve as you learn from customers what their opinion is and how it changes over time because their preferences and expectations will change as new and different things are offered by other companies. With new competitors, new trends, and new and different ways to communicate with customers occurring regularly, what once signaled a trustworthy service can change, resulting in a loss of customers for no apparent reason.

Examples that change how customers perceive the riskiness or trustworthiness of your services can be the introduction of online booking by competitors, the adoption of credit card terminals, an increase in open operating hours, a reduction in delivery costs or times, contact or support details listed for easy customer use, or even having a website or being transparent about pricing. After all, if competitors are showing pricing online and your business isn't, it can make customers question whether you are hiding something or have overly complicated or discriminatory pricing.

Next, to decide and prioritize ongoing improvements to improve your services, find out what your customers prefer and think about your business compared to your competitors. You can do this by asking them through surveys or reading reviews they give during the service or after using a product in person or online. Then, use this information to make changes that will better meet your customers' needs.

Next, train your employees to learn what customers say and share it with you as the owner or manager. Ensure that they know how to communicate effectively with customers. Training should include skills such as active listening, problem-solving, and empathy.

Other ways to encourage customers to share their opinions on your business are by offering ways for them to give feedback. For example, you can use online review platforms or put a suggestion box at your location. Getting feedback will help you learn where you can improve.

4.2 Small Steps to Big Impact: Embracing Incremental Improvement

In this chapter, I'll show you how small service businesses like yours can make small, ongoing changes to stay relevant and meet your customers' needs. This process, called incremental improvement, helps you keep up with the changes being made by competitors and other companies that change what customers want or expect from a business like yours and set your business apart from the competition.

Vital ways to performing incremental improvements that will be attractive to your most profitable customers is to first do your research, then brainstorm and evaluate the ideas you learned from the research, then test them to find out if they do attract more and better customers, and above all, stay committed to improvements. I'll go through each in the following sections.

Do Your Research

Do research to understand your customers' needs and preferences. Preference research will help you come up with new ideas and improve your existing products and services. It's easy to see what people say online about companies and their needs. Search for your company name or the name of your competitors and read any reviews or mentions of the company by customers.

Preference research is about finding out what your customers like or don't like and what they wish a product or service was, is, or could be. It's like listening to what people say about what they want or need. For a small business owner, this can help you make your products or services better. You can find out what people enjoy and what they are not happy with. Maybe they want something made in a different way or a service that does something special. By understanding these things, you can change what you offer to make your customers happier and your business more successful. Here are some ways to do your research:

Online poll for service enhancement: If you run a small salon and are considering introducing online booking for customers, you could create a poll on your social media page or website asking customers if this were something they would like. By asking a simple question like, "Would you prefer to book your appointments online?" you can gauge interest and make an informed decision.

Customer interviews for product improvement: If you have a small bakery and want to introduce new flavors, you could conduct short interviews with regular customers. Ask them what flavors they enjoy, what they wish you offered, or what they think could be improved. Their insights can guide your menu expansion and ensure that you're offering items that are appealing to your customers.

Observation and feedback for operational changes: If you own a small retail store and notice that customers seem to have difficulty finding certain items, you could observe their shopping behavior and ask for feedback. Understanding where they struggle can help you rearrange the store layout or add signage to improve the shopping experience.

These examples of preference research show how listening to customers and actively seeking their input can lead to meaningful improvements in products, services, and overall operations. By tuning into what customers like, dislike, or wish for, you can make targeted changes that enhance satisfaction and contribute to the success of your micro business.

Brainstorm and Evaluate Ideas

After identifying your customers' wants, brainstorm new ideas for your products and services. First, focus on ideas that match your strengths and expertise. Then, evaluate which ones are feasible and profitable.

Brainstorm and evaluate ideas: After researching your customers' preferences, it's time to brainstorm and evaluate ideas that cater to those specific likes and dislikes. Here are three simple techniques for micro business owners:

Mind mapping: Start with the preferences you've identified and draw branches with related product or service ideas.

Mind mapping example for a gardening store: Suppose you run a small gardening store and have identified that customers prefer organic products. You could start with "Organic Gardening" at the center of your mind map and draw branches to related ideas such as "Organic Soil," "Organic Plant Food," "Organic Pest Control," and "Organic Seeds." Each of these branches could further branch into specific products or services you could offer.

Rapid listing: Write down as many ideas as you can that align with customer needs. Don't judge them yet; just let the ideas flow.

Rapid listing example for a café: If you own a small café and have learned that customers are looking for healthier menu options, you could quickly list ideas such as "Vegan Sandwiches," "Gluten-Free Pastries," "Fresh Juice Bar," "Salad Bowls with Local Ingredients," "Low-Calorie Smoothies," and so on. The goal is to jot down as many ideas as possible without overthinking them, allowing creativity to flow.

The "What If" technique: Ask yourself "What if?" questions based on customer preferences and explore different scenarios.

The "What If" technique example for an auto repair shop: Imagine you have a small auto repair shop, and customers have expressed a desire for more transparent pricing. You could ask yourself questions like "What if I offered a detailed price breakdown for each service?" or "What if I created package deals for common repairs?" or "What if I provided a price match guarantee?" Exploring these scenarios can lead to innovative solutions that match customer preferences.

These examples demonstrate how the techniques of mind mapping, rapid listing, and the "What If" technique can be applied to both product-based and service-based micro businesses. By starting with customer preferences and using these methods, you can generate creative and relevant ideas to enhance your offerings and meet customer needs.

Once you've brainstormed, evaluate the ideas by considering your resources, time, and budget. Think about what fits your business best and what matches what your customers have said they want. Look for ideas that you can realistically implement and that have the potential to satisfy your customers' preferences and grow your business. Sometimes, a simple idea that directly responds to a customer's wish can be the most impactful.

Test your ideas: Before introducing your new ideas to the market, it's essential to test them to make sure they work well and meet customer needs. Here are ways you can do this:

Product or service testing:

- Small group testing: Select a small group of loyal customers and offer them a sample or trial of the new product or service.
- Online poll or survey: Use social media or e-mail to run a poll or survey, targeting actual customers.
- In-store or virtual demonstration: Host a demonstration of the new product or service either in your physical store or through a virtual platform.

Service, operational, and administrative improvements:

- Service improvement: Test a new scheduling system that allows customers to book and manage appointments online.
- Operational improvement: Implement a new method of managing inventory to reduce waste and track the results.
- Administrative improvement: Explore a new CRM system that helps you track sales and customer interactions more effectively.

Remember, when using social media or e-mail for feedback, it's important to target actual customers to ensure you receive relevant and practical insights. By testing your ideas with real customers, whether they are related to products, services, operations, or administration, you can make informed decisions and refine your offerings to better align with what your customers truly want and need. This comprehensive approach ensures that all aspects of your business match what customers need, thereby improving your financial performance.

Stay Committed to Improvement

To make small changes better over time, you need to keep looking for ways to improve. This means looking at everything, not just the things you sell. Think about how people find out about your business, how they buy from you, how you help them if they have questions, and how you thank them after they buy.

For example, maybe people like what you sell but find it hard to pay on your website. Making this easier can make them happier. Or maybe they like your service but wish it was easier to park near your shop. Fixing this can make them want to come back. If you have a small restaurant, maybe people wish you had a menu in another language. Adding this can make more people want to eat at your place.

Keep watching what people like and what is popular in the market. Ask your customers what they think, look at what people say online, and see what other businesses like yours are doing. Try to make every part of dealing with your business better, not just the products or services you sell. By doing this, you can make sure your small business stays strong and gives your customers what they want and need.

In conclusion, incremental improvement is essential for small service businesses like yours to stay appealing and relevant. By researching the market, developing, testing new ideas, and committing to ongoing improvement, you can substantially enhance how you run your business, your products, and services, and increase your financial performance.

4.3 Success in Action: The Small Animal Care Clinic's Journey to Continuous Improvement

Creating and maintaining a continuous improvement strategy is essential for any business's success, especially for small service companies. This chapter will provide a case study of a small animal care clinic's successful continuous improvement strategy. We will explore the steps they took to adapt to changes in the market, connect with their community, and improve their business performance, including specific strategies they implemented, such as revamping their online presence and adjusting their approach to animal care.

Background of the company: The small service company we will examine is an animal care clinic. A veterinarian started the business with 22 years of experience in traditional and holistic animal care. Despite his expertise, he faced challenges entering a new community with several established animal care providers. As a result, the clinic struggled to demonstrate its superiority and attract new customers.

Recognizing the need for change: The vet consulted me, a customer of the clinic, to adapt to the local market. Together, we analyzed the competition and the pet care preferences of local pet owners.

Adapting to market changes: The team conducted informal research to understand the area's preferences for pet care services and identified areas for improvement. We then revamped the clinic's online presence, website, social media, and Google My Business page to create a consistent and appealing business personality that reflected the community's needs. Next, the clinic staff adjusted their approach to engaging with animals, treating them as family members to build trust and interest in the new clinic.

Monitoring the progress: The clinic owner continuously learned new marketing methods and adapted to changes in the business environment, becoming more relevant and preferred in the community. In addition, by focusing on a unique business personality and offering holistic treatments alongside traditional ones, they set themselves apart from the competition.

Results of the company's adaptation: As a result of these changes, the clinic saw a dramatic increase in customers, loyalty from existing clients, and increased revenue and profitability. After this initial adaptation, the vet has continued to adapt as the business environment around him is changing. This business has been operating successfully for over 12 years.

This animal care clinic's success story underlines the importance of adapting to market changes and continually monitoring progress to ensure the business remains relevant and effective. By setting goals, collecting data, and making informed decisions based on the feedback and results, the clinic continues fine-tuning its continuous improvement strategies to ensure sustained success.

In conclusion, this case study exemplifies how recognizing the need for change, adapting to market shifts, creating a strong business personality, and rigorously monitoring progress can lead to a tremendous positive impact on business performance.

4.4 The Power of Continuous Improvement and Innovation: Key Insights and Next Steps

This chapter explored the importance of continuous improvement and innovation for small service companies. By enhancing service delivery, implementing incremental improvements, and adapting to customer preferences, small businesses can set themselves apart from competitors and increase their performance. I outlined practical steps to achieve these improvements.

The case study of a local animal care clinic highlighted the benefits of continuous improvement, such as improved customer experience, loyalty, and revenue. You can significantly improve your business performance by following this example and incorporating the practical steps discussed.

Here are some key takeaways to enhance your business performance:

Engage with current and potential customers: Actively seeking customer feedback and insights helps drive continuous improvement, leading to better services and increased customer loyalty.

Invest in employee training: Regular training enables employees to deliver relevant customer experiences and stay informed about industry trends and techniques.

Use data and analysis: Customer research helps you refine your company, services, and products to stay relevant as the market changes.

Invest in continual improvements: Frequently improving and sharing information with customers improves revenue significantly.

To implement these takeaways, you can begin by identifying areas for improvement in service delivery and introducing incremental changes. Regularly gathering feedback from customers and employees provides valuable insights for further improvement. You can progress toward your goals and maintain relevance in your market as you collect information to make ongoing improvements.

In the next chapter, I'll discuss the significance of business personality for small service companies and offer practical steps for building a solid business personality that is attractive to customers.

4.5 Start: Use Customer Feedback for Continuous Growth

Listening to what customers say and making changes based on their feedback is very important for a business that wants to keep growing. It provides invaluable insights into customer experiences, preferences, and expectations, enabling businesses to adapt, improve, and grow. This project is crucial as it offers a structured approach to use customer feedback for continuous growth.

In this brief, we explore ways to effectively collect, analyze, and implement changes based on customer feedback to enhance your business.

Objectives

This project aims to establish a systematic approach to gather, analyze, and use customer feedback to improve service delivery and enhance customer experience.

Scope

- Identification of relevant online platforms for customer reviews
- Regular monitoring and analysis of customer reviews
- Professional and prompt response to customer reviews
- Development and implementation of an action plan based on feedback
- Communication of improvements to customers

Deliverables

- A list of relevant online platforms for customer reviews
- A schedule for regular monitoring of customer reviews
- A process for responding to customer reviews
- An action plan based on customer feedback
- A communication plan to share improvements with customers

Timeline

- Week 1: Identification of relevant online platforms
- Week 2: Planning to check things regularly and deciding how to respond
- Weeks 3 to 4: Monitoring and analysis of customer reviews
- Week 5: Development of action plan
- Weeks 6 to 8: Implementation of action plan
- Week 9: Development of communication plan
- Week 10: Communication of improvements to customers

Resources Required

- Access to online review platforms
- Dedicated personnel for monitoring and responding to reviews
- Resources for implementing changes based on feedback
- Communication tools for sharing improvements with customers

Risks and Challenges

- Inability to monitor all review platforms
- Negative reviews and handling customer dissatisfaction
- Implementing changes based on diverse and sometimes conflicting feedback
- Communicating improvements effectively to customers

Key Stakeholders

- Business owner
- Employees involved in service delivery
- Customers providing feedback
- Personnel responsible for monitoring and responding to reviews
- Personnel responsible for implementing changes based on feedback

Step 1: Recognize the Need for Collecting and Using Customer Feedback

Recognizing the need for collecting and using customer feedback is your first step toward improving your business. Customer feedback is not just about identifying areas for improvement in your products or services but also about gaining a deeper understanding of your customer's needs, preferences, and expectations. This understanding can guide your decisions and help you create a customer experience that matches your customers' needs.

Why Customer Feedback Matters

According to Microsoft, 96 percent of people say how they are treated is a factor in which companies they are loyal. This statistic highlights the importance of understanding and meeting your customers' needs.

Moreover, a study by Esteban Kolsky found that 91 percent of customers who are unhappy with a company will leave without complaining. This study shows you might never know why you lose customers without actively seeking customer feedback.

Plus, online surveys show that close to 100 percent (0.94) say they avoid a business because of negative reviews. This statistic highlights the impact of unresolved or nonresponded negative reviews on a business's reputation and the chance of getting new customers. It also highlights the potential consequences of not actively engaging in this project if you aren't managing customer feedback.

Recognizing the Need

The need for collecting and using customer feedback can become apparent in various situations. For instance, if you own a small bakery, you might recognize the need for this project when:

> You notice a decrease in repeat customers: If your regular customers stop coming, it could be a sign that they're unsatisfied with your products or service. Collecting feedback can help you understand what's going wrong and how to fix it.

You receive a negative review: Negative reviews offer valuable insights into business improvement areas. However, it's important to remember that not all customers will leave reviews, so actively asking for feedback is crucial.

A new competitor enters the market: When a new bakery opens in your area, it's a good idea to collect feedback to understand how your offerings compare to theirs and what you can do to show your business is relevant. It's also common for your customers to try out other new competitors; so, don't panic if there is a dip in business. Often competition increases customers as long as you stay relevant.

The Risks of Ignoring Customer Feedback

Loss of customers: If customers feel that their or other customers, opinions, and concerns are not heard, they may choose to take their business elsewhere.

Missed opportunities for improvement: Without customer feedback, you might miss out on opportunities to improve your products, services, or overall customer experience.

Damage to your reputation: Unaddressed negative feedback can harm your business's reputation, especially in the age of social media, where negative reviews can quickly spread.

In conclusion, recognizing the need for collecting and using customer feedback is a crucial first step in improving your business and enhancing your customer experience. By actively asking for and replying to feedback, you build a strong relationship with customers, improve your products, services, and overall experience, and ultimately, drive your business's success.

Step 2: Communicate

Effective communication is critical to managing and improving your customer experience. Online reviews are one of the most direct ways to communicate with your customers. These reviews provide a wealth of information about your customers' experiences, needs, and expectations.

Choosing and Joining the Right Platforms

Businesses will find different platforms more relevant based on their industry and customer base. For instance, if you own a restaurant, platforms such as Yelp and Google My Business are likely the most appropriate as they are commonly used for reviewing dining experiences. On the other hand, if you sell handmade crafts, reviews on your Etsy shop or Facebook page might be more pertinent.

To identify the right platforms for your business, consider where your customers are most active and where they are most likely to leave reviews. You can do this by surveying your customers, researching industry trends, or even observing where your competitors are receiving reviews.

However, ensuring they are direct competitors is crucial when considering your competitors' platforms. For instance, if you're a small regional bakery, it would be beneficial to be on the same review platforms as other small regional bakeries. But if your competitor is a large national chain, their platforms might not be as relevant to your customer base.

Once you've identified the most relevant platforms, creating a business account on these platforms is essential if you haven't already. A business account makes it easier for customers to review your company and allows you to respond directly.

Focus on Online Customer Reviews

It's also crucial to consider the impact of zero-click searches. A zero-click search means the answer to the user's search terms or keywords appears at the top of the search results page. The user doesn't need to click a link to get the information. In the context of online reviews, this means that when potential customers search for your business, they can see and read your Google reviews directly from the search results page. They don't need to click on your website or Google My Business page.

Reviews are highly visible and influential. They are used to determine whether a potential customer will use your business. Most small business owners rely on word-of-mouth as a primary source of new customers but don't recognize that online reviews are also word-of-mouth. The same way they respond to customers in person or via e-mail or chat is the same way they should respond to public reviews. If your reviews are mostly positive, this can help attract new customers. If your reviews are all positive—5/5, it signals that they may be false.

While you might think that all positive reviews are what you strive for, the truth is, as customers, we expect some customers to be unhappy with a service or product, so a few negative comments are expected. We are suspicious that the positive reviews are fake when we don't see any less than 5/5. Don't fear negative reviews; respond to them positively to show everyone looking at your reviews that you are a responsive and legitimate company.

Negative reviews stop potential customers from trying your business if they are not responded to or addressed. Therefore, it's crucial to communicate effectively and manage your online reviews, particularly on Google. Monitor your reviews, respond to them promptly and professionally, and use the feedback to make necessary improvements to your business.

ReviewTrackers say 65 percent of desktop searches result in zero-click searches in 2020. This statistic highlights the importance of managing your online reputation, particularly on Google, as potential customers can see your reviews directly from the search results page. This means that even if you try to manage your reviews to hide negative ones, zero-click searches will display your reviews directly in the search results. Potential customers can see these without having to visit your website, selling site, or social media pages.

Monitoring Online Reviews

After setting up your business accounts, the next step is regularly monitoring these platforms for new reviews. Monitoring can be done manually by setting aside time each week to check each platform. However, a more efficient method is using tools such as Google Alerts that automatically notify you of new mentions of your business online.

Setting Up Google Alerts

Google Alerts sends free e-mail notifications whenever your business is mentioned online. Here's a simple template for setting up Google Alerts:

1. Go to www.google.com/alerts
2. Enter your business name or other relevant keywords in the "Create an alert about" box. Keywords could include your name, service, product names, or anything else people might use to refer to your business online
3. Click "Show options." Here, you can specify how often you want to receive alerts, the types of sites you want Google to search, and other options
4. Click "Create Alert"

After you have set up the alert, you will receive a link in an e-mail to any mention. Creating an alert allows you to monitor what people say quickly and easily about your business online and respond to any feedback or reviews as necessary.

Remember, communication is a two-way street. Replying to positive and negative online reviews shows customers you appreciate them and are committed to improving their experience—whether you agree with the feedback. Responding not only helps improve your business but also builds trust and loyalty among your customers.

Step 3: Involve Your Team

Regularly monitor reviews. ReviewTracker says that review interaction is up by 50 percent from prepandemic levels. It's one of the many signs demonstrating people's heightened sensitivities about where to go or what to purchase in the wake of the pandemic. Regularly monitoring reviews should be a weekly task you can assign to a specific task member if you aren't using review tracking software.

Example: If you run a small online clothing store with a team of three, you could assign one person to monitor and compile a weekly report of online reviews.

Table 4.1 Example of compiling weekly online review report

Date	Platform	Customer Name	Rating	Review Summary	Response Needed?	Response Given
7/1/2023	Google My Business	John Doe	5 stars	Loved the friendly service and quick delivery	Thank you	Responded on 7/1/2023
7/2/2023	Yelp	Jane Smith	3 stars	Good product, but delivery took longer than expected	Apologise	Responded on 7/3/2023
7/3/2023	Facebook	Bob Johnson	2 stars	Product arrived damaged	Apology, return and resend	Responded on 7/3/2023

Here's an example of how you might compile a weekly report of online reviews.

In this report (Table 4.1), you can track the review date, the platform it was left on, the customer's name, their rating, a summary of their review, the response needed, and when the reply has been given. Monitoring reviews will help you keep track of your online reputation and ensure you're responding to feedback on time.

Look at review tracking software such as ReviewTrackers, BirdEye, or Podium that combines review sites, so you don't have to manage multiple logins.

Remember, the key to using these tools effectively is to regularly monitor your reviews and respond promptly and professionally. Professional responses show you appreciate hearing customers' opinions and are prompt in responding.

Step 4: Provide Resources and Training

Train yourself and your team on how to manage reviews. The following ReviewTracker statistics show the need for training staff on effectively responding to customer reviews in a way that shows care and concern for the customer's experience.

- Just over half of the people, 53.3 percent, expect a response to their online reviews within seven days, and 30 percent expect a reply within three days

- Not replying to reviews risks increasing customer loss by up to 15 percent
- Replying to negative reviews increases potential customers by 45 percent

These abovementioned statistics emphasize the importance of not just monitoring reviews but also responding to them in a timely and effective manner. Monitoring involves creating guidelines and scripts for responding to positive and negative feedback.

Guidelines for Responding to Customer Feedback

Acknowledge the feedback: Start by thanking the customer for taking the time to provide feedback. Gratitude shows that you value their opinion and are open to hearing their thoughts. Example: "Thank you for taking the time to share your feedback with us."

Address the customer by name: Personalize your response by addressing the customer by name. Using their name makes the answer feel more personal and shows the customer they are not just another number. Example: "Dear [Customer's Name],"

Show empathy: If the feedback is negative, show empathy and understanding. Compassion shows the customer that you care about their experience and take their concerns seriously. Example: "We're sorry to hear you had a less than satisfactory experience."

Address the feedback directly: Respond to the specific points raised in the feedback. Show the customer that you have read and understood their feedback. Example: "We understand you were disappointed with [specific issue]."

Provide a solution or next steps: If possible, provide a solution to the problem or explain how you will fix the problem. Offering a solution shows the customer that you are committed to improving their experience. Example: "We have addressed this issue with our team and are working on a solution."

Invite further communication: Encourage the customer to reach out if they have any other concerns or questions. Show that you are open to further communication and are committed to improving their experience. Example: "If you have any other concerns or questions, please don't hesitate to contact us."

Close on a positive note: End your response on a positive note, thanking the customer again for their feedback and expressing your commitment to improving their experience. Example: "Thank you again for your feedback. We are committed to improving our services and your experience."

Scripts Example

Positive review response template: "Hi [Customer's Name], thank you so much for your kind words! We're thrilled to hear you enjoyed [specific detail from their review]. We look forward to serving you again soon!"

Negative review response template: "Hi [Customer's Name], we're sorry to hear about your experience. We take your feedback seriously and want to understand more about what happened. Could you please contact us at [your contact information] so we can address this issue?"

Responding to customer feedback shows the customer that you value their opinion and are seriously committed to improving their experience. By following these guidelines, you can effectively respond and build stronger customer relationships.

Step 5: Refine and Adjust as Necessary

Based on the feedback gathered from customer reviews, identify areas where you can improve your business.

Example: If you own a pet grooming service and several reviews mentioned long wait times, you might decide to hire an additional groomer or implement an appointment system.

Let's say you've identified a need to improve your customer service response time. Here's a step-by-step guide on how to implement this improvement:

Identify your needs: Determine what you need to improve your customer service response time. Do you need more customer service representatives? Do you need to implement new customer service software? Or do you need to provide additional training to your current team?

Research options: There are many ways to improve customer service response time. You could hire additional staff, implement new customer service software such as Zendesk or Freshdesk, or provide extra training to your current team on efficient response strategies.

Consider customer experience: Choose an option to improve response time and enhance the customer experience. The goal is to respond to customers quickly and ensure that you resolve their issues satisfactorily.

Test the improvement: Before fully implementing the new improvement, test it. Monitor response times and customer effort levels to ensure the modification has the desired effect.

Train your team: Make sure you train everyone who will be affected by the improvement of the new processes. They should understand the why and how of the improvement to effectively implement it.

Communicate the change to customers: Let your customers know about the improvement. You can do this through an e-mail announcement, a post on your website, or a sign in your physical location (if applicable). This transparency can increase customer trust and loyalty.

Gather feedback: After implementing the improvement, ask your customers for feedback. Are they noticing a difference in response times? Are their issues being resolved more efficiently? Use this feedback to make continuous improvements.

Remember, the goal of any improvement is to enhance the customer experience and meet your business needs. By considering your needs and the customer experience, you can implement a modification that will benefit your business.

Step 6: Celebrate Success and Learn From Failure

Sharing improvements with your customers is a crucial step in the feedback process. Sharing not only shows your customers that you value their feedback but also shows that you are committed to improving their experience. Share through various channels such as social media posts, e-mail newsletters, and direct communication.

For instance, you could post an update on your social media platforms saying, "Thanks to your valuable feedback, we've made some exciting changes! We've expanded our team by hiring an additional groomer to reduce wait times. Book your appointment today and let us know what you think of the improvements!"

In addition to celebrating successes, it's equally important to learn from failures. Negative reviews are useful information for understanding where your business may fall short of customer expectations. Remember, almost half of potential customers ignore negative reviews if you have responded to them. This statistic underscores the importance of addressing and learning from negative feedback.

Moreover, 80 percent of people think a business cares about them when management responds to their reviews. This statistic emphasizes the importance of learning from failure and its impact on your business's reputation and customer loyalty.

In conclusion, celebrate your victories, learn from your mistakes, and continuously improving your business based on customer feedback. It's about showing your current and potential customers that their opinion matters and that you're committed to providing them with the best possible experience.

4.6 Plan: Improve Your Customer Experience Through Owner and Employee Training

Customer experience training is vital to consistently delivering relevant customer experiences. Equipping yourself and your employees with the necessary skills and knowledge can reduce customer effort, foster loyalty, and drive business growth.

In this brief, we explore the importance of customer experience training and provide practical steps for you to invest in training programs that align with your specific needs.

Objectives

Our objectives for this project brief are to:

- Highlight the significance of customer experience training for small business owners
- Provide actionable steps to identify training needs and select appropriate programs
- Establish a regular training schedule to ensure continuous improvement

Scope

- Assessing areas of customer experience that require improvement
- Identifying relevant training programs based on specific business needs
- Developing a regular training schedule to maintain new skills

Deliverables

- A comprehensive understanding of the importance of customer experience training
- Guidelines for identifying training needs and selecting appropriate programs
- Recommendations for establishing a regular training schedule to foster continuous improvement

Timeline

- Assessing training needs: One week
- Researching and selecting training programs: Two weeks
- Establishing a regular training schedule: Ongoing, with monthly or quarterly sessions

Resources Required

- Access to online resources and training program databases
- Time for researching and selecting training programs

- Training facilities or virtual platforms for conducting sessions
- Training materials and resources provided by chosen programs

Risks and Challenges

- Limited availability of suitable training programs within budget constraints
- Potential resistance or reluctance from employees to engage in training
- Balancing training schedules with daily business operations

Key Stakeholders

- Small business owners
- Employees
- Training program providers
- Customers

Step 1: Recognize the Need for Investing in Training

Knowing how important customer experience is to business is vital today. Many small business owners don't realize how much it can affect their success. Here are some facts to consider:

Keeping customers: When you keep just 5 percent more customers, you could make 25 percent to 95 percent more money. Training on how to make customers happy helps with this.

Customers pay more for better service: Some studies show that 43 percent of people will pay more if it's easier to buy something. And 42 percent will pay more if the people selling it are friendly. Training on how to treat customers can help make this happen.

Happy customers tell others: If a customer likes what you do, they will tell about it to nine other people. If they don't like it, they will tell 16 people. Training on how to make customers happy helps make sure more people hear good things about your business. Most small business owners still use or learn about the 4Ps (Product, Price,

Place, and Promotion). This way of thinking is old and doesn't include everything needed to make customers happy every time they buy something. Even though it's out-of-date, many schools and universities still teach it because it's simple and changing textbooks costs money.

This gap in knowledge shows the urgent need for proper training, especially for businesses that provide services. That's because things like the people who work there, the way things are done, and what customers see and feel are important but not part of the 4Ps. Investing in the right training helps business owners understand these essential aspects that are often talked about in new ways to market services but aren't in the 4Ps.

You should know that customer experience isn't about always being amazing; it's about giving a steady experience that keeps a fair deal between you and your customers. This deal is like an agreement between you and them. You promise things such as good service, quality products, quick responses, clear communication, and fair prices. They give you their money in return.

Both sides get something good from this deal—you offer something valuable, and they pay for it. In this agreement, you meet your customers' needs and wants, and it can include different things, from simple to fancy, slow to quick, or cheap to expensive. What matters most is that you keep your promises all the time, so your customers get what they expect and think it's worth it. This fair deal helps build trust and shows that you take your work seriously. Think of this fair deal as the customer experience itself.

New businesses typically start with a fair deal that customers experience, but during slow periods they often make changes to cut costs without fully appreciating that these changes may alter the customer experience, making it inconsistent and potentially worse. Even if customers don't consciously notice the changes, subconsciously, they may sense that something isn't quite right or not as good as before. Reduced experiences can initiate a downward spiral for the business.

New business owners sometimes also make the mistake of considering their customers as friends who will understand any changes in the experience during slow periods. However, customers are not friends, and you shouldn't expect them to empathize with the challenges of running a small business. They pay for an experience that is consistent and valuable each time they interact with the company.

Recognizing the need to invest in customer experience training is crucial for ensuring you understand the importance of consistency and can implement strategies to deliver a reliable customer experience. By prioritizing consistent customer experiences, you can increase customer loyalty, repeat business, and encourage positive word-of-mouth recommendations.

Step 2: Communicate

Effective communication plays a vital role in implementing customer experience training. Here are two critical aspects of communication to consider:

> Internal communication: Communicate the importance of customer experience training to your team. Explain how it will benefit both the business and the customers. Emphasize the significance of their participation and encourage them to share ideas and feedback with you. When addressing the team:
> - "You are crucial in delivering a consistent and valuable customer experience. By providing our promised service and maintaining sameness, we can get customers to come back more often and tell their friends and family about our business, which will help us grow."
> - "Let's focus on creating an experience our customers can rely on. Our dedication to sameness will set us apart from the competition and encourage our customers to choose us time and time again."
> - "Your participation in customer experience training is vital. It will give you additional skills to meet our customer expectations while providing a consistent experience matching our business values."
> By effectively communicating the importance of customer experience training to the team and customers you can create a shared under-

standing and commitment to delivering a consistent and valuable experience. Your business will benefit by creating customers who trust and appreciate your value.

Customer communication: Tell customers about the improvements you are making through training initiatives. Communicate via social media, e-mail newsletters, or in-person discussions to highlight the steps you are taking to enhance their experience.

When speaking to customers:

- "Thank you for choosing our business. We are committed to providing you with a consistent experience that you can rely on each time you visit. We value your business and want to ensure your experience meets our promise."
- "We know that you want the same service from us every time. So, we work hard to give you what we promise, no matter what happens."
- "Our goal is to make it easy for you to keep coming back and to recommend us to your friends and family. We are grateful for your trust and want to ensure that every experience you have with our business leaves a positive impression."

Encourage customers to provide feedback and let them know their opinions are valued.

Step 3: Involve Your Team

Involving your team in the customer experience training process creates a sense of ownership and commitment. Use team involvement, hold idea-sharing sessions, training sessions, or role-playing scenarios. For example:

Team involvement: Create opportunities for your employees to actively participate in the training process. Encourage them to share their insights, experiences, and suggestions for improving customer experience based on their interactions with customers. Make sure everyone feels comfortable contributing their ideas from their customer experiences.

Idea-sharing sessions: Hold a meeting where everyone can talk about their experiences with customers. You could do this once a month at the end of the workday or during a lunch break. The important thing is to make sure everyone gets a chance to speak and that you consider all ideas relevant to customer experiences. You can keep track of the ideas in a notebook or on a computer.

Step 4: Provide Resources and Training

Here are three steps you can take to invest in training for yourself and your employees:

Determine the type of training needed: Start by assessing the areas of customer experience that need improvement.

Critical Customer Experience Areas

a. Customer service: This includes how you respond to customer inquiries, handle complaints, and help. It's about being helpful, friendly, efficient, and delivering on your service promises.
b. Product or service quality: How well your product or service meets customer expectations based on what you promised.
c. Ease of doing business: This includes how easy it is for customers to find information, make purchases, and get support. It's about making things simple and convenient for your customers.
d. Customer communication: This refers to how well you keep customers informed about your products, services, and any changes or updates. It's about being clear, transparent, and timely in your communication.

Then, consider the feedback you've received from customers, such as online reviews or customer effort surveys, to identify improvement areas.

Common Feedback and Interpretation

a. "Your staff is always helpful and friendly": This is positive feedback about your customer service. Keep doing what you're doing!

b. "I love your product, but it's always out of stock": This is feedback about your product quality and availability. You might need to improve your inventory management.

c. "Your website is hard to navigate": This is feedback about the ease of doing business. You might need to improve your website design.

d. "I didn't know about your new product until it was sold out": This is feedback about your customer communication. You might need to improve how you inform customers about new products or updates.

Once you've identified these areas, look for training programs that specialize in them.

Choose the Right Training Program

With thousands available, choosing a training program can be overwhelming. Look for affordable programs, provide flexible scheduling, and have positive reviews from previous participants. Also, ensure that the training program is relevant to your business and the skills you want to improve.

Training Program Keywords

Based on the abovementioned areas and feedback, you might search for training programs using keywords such as "customer service training," "product quality control training," "website usability training," or "customer communication training."

Example Training Program for Limited Resources

If resources are limited, consider free or low-cost online courses. Websites such as YouTube, Coursera, Udemy, and Khan Academy.

Your investment in customer experience training will enhance customer interactions, improve customer experience, and drive business success.

Here is a practical training suggestion for a service business:

Service business: Train employees on effective customer communication and problem-solving skills. A training program focusing on empathy, conflict resolution, and active listening can help employees provide valued customer service.

Establish a regular training schedule: Customer experience training is not a one-time event. Over time, customer expectations may change as the external business environment does, so what currently is considered valued customer experience may be different tomorrow. For example:

January: Kick-off meeting to discuss the importance of customer experience, review customer feedback from the previous year, and set goals for the year.

February: Training Session 1—"Improving Customer Service." Identify issues common among customers to be discussed on how to resolve. Methods could involve role-playing exercises based on actual customer interactions.

Establishing a regular training schedule is essential to maintain the skills and knowledge gained in training. Consider scheduling monthly or quarterly training sessions for employees to continue building their skills and knowledge.

Step 5: Refine and Adjust as Necessary

Continuous improvement is vital for maintaining a consistent customer experience. After identifying your team's customer experience training needs and implementing the initial training, it's essential to refine and adjust the program to ensure ongoing success. Here are two key considerations:

Analyze feedback on training effectiveness: Regularly review feedback from both customers and team members to identify areas where the training may need refinement. Look for recurring themes or suggestions, as these are valuable inputs for fine-tuning the training strategies.

- Coffee shop: If customers repeatedly mention the coffee is too cold, assess whether the team needs further training on the equipment.

Track important numbers relating to training impact: Decide on specific metrics that show how well the training is affecting customer experience. Analyze these numbers to see if the training is achieving its goals. If not, figure out what's going wrong and adjust the training. For example:

- Hair salon: If fewer clients are returning, evaluate if the training on delivering a consistent experience is effective.

These examples illustrate how both human-related and product-related aspects can influence the customer experience, emphasizing the need to continuously refine training to address these areas. By closely monitoring feedback and key numbers, you can ensure that your team's customer experience training remains effective and matches your business's needs and values.

Step 6: Celebrate Success and Learn From Failure

By identifying the type of training needed, choosing the right training program, and establishing a regular training schedule, you can provide a customer experience that delivers its promise and grows the business. When you introduce a training program that makes the customer experience consistent, it's important to celebrate this achievement. Here is a simple and low-cost way to do this:

> Team lunch or dinner: Consider having a team meal to celebrate after completing a training program. A meal doesn't have to be expensive—it could be a potluck where everyone brings a dish to share, or you could order pizza. Use this time to acknowledge everyone's hard work and discuss the positive changes you hope to see in customer experience.

Learning From Failure

Even with the best intentions, sometimes training programs don't have the desired impact. Three common issues to look out for are lack of engagement, no follow up, and ignoring feedback. For example:

> Lack of engagement: If your team members aren't participating or interested during the training, they're unlikely to learn and apply

what they've learned. To avoid this, ensure that the training is inter-active and relevant to their work. Ask for their input when choosing a training program and include plenty of opportunities for discussion and practice during the training.

4.7 Do: Uncovering Profitable Customer Needs for Business Growth

This project is integral to your business growth. It enables you to understand and effectively serve your customers, uncovering their preferences. The insights gained will shape your marketing strategy, allowing you to target your products and services more precisely and foster stronger relationships with your customers.

In this brief, we explore three simple yet effective ways for gathering customer feedback: conducting customer surveys, monitoring social media, and analyzing customer purchase history.

Objectives

Gather actionable customer feedback and use this information to improve your marketing strategy and business growth.

Scope

- Creation and implementation of customer surveys
- Monitoring and analysis of social media interactions
- Study of customer purchase history

Deliverables

- Comprehensive customer survey report
- Social media monitoring report
- Analysis report of customer purchase history

Timeline

- Customer survey development and deployment: One to two weeks

- Social media monitoring: Ongoing, with monthly report preparation
- Purchase history analysis: Ongoing, with quarterly report preparation

Resources Required

- Online survey tools
- Social media monitoring tools
- Sales receipt tracking system

Risks and Challenges

- Difficulty in reaching a significant portion of your customer base for surveys
- Interpretation of raw social media information into actionable activities
- Ensuring privacy and security in storing and analyzing customer purchase history

Key Stakeholders

- Business owner
- Marketing person (internal or contract)
- Customer service person (internal or contract)
- Data analysis person (internal or contract)

Step 1: Recognize the Need to Uncover Customer's Preferences

You might think you thoroughly understand your customers, especially if your customer base is small. However, customers' preferences can change, and new customers may have different needs. You might think you thoroughly understand your customers, especially if your customer base is small. However, customers' preferences can change, and new customers may have different needs. For example, a Thai restaurant owner in Vancouver thought his unique selling point was sourcing ingredients directly from Thailand. But as the community changed, this feature lost its appeal. Another restaurant owner chose a location based on affordability but tried to impose his cooking style, which didn't align with local preferences. Both businesses suffered because they didn't adapt to their changing customer base.

Interestingly, research shows that while most business owners attribute the decline or closure of their business to changes in their environment, the real issue often lies in their inability to adapt to those changes. It's easy to fall into the trap of believing that what has worked in the past will continue to work. As neighborhoods evolve and new trends emerge, your once-loyal customers might start looking for different things. Ignoring these shifts and sticking to your old ways can lead to a decline in business. Therefore, it's essential to regularly reassess customer preferences and be willing to adjust to stay relevant.

Understand Your Local Community Changes

Customers' preferences can change significantly with shifts in community demographics. As neighborhoods evolve, with an average of 30 percent change in some areas yearly, new families, singles, and older adults may move in, each bringing unique needs and tastes. These demographic shifts mean new customers with different preferences. For example, a younger demographic might prefer digital transactions and trendy products or takeaways, while an older population might prioritize personalized service and traditional goods. Therefore, it's crucial to remain aware of these shifts and continually reassess customer preferences to accommodate these changes.

Recognize the Impact of Lifestyle and Age-Related Changes

Demographic shifts, lifestyle changes, and the natural progression of aging can also influence customer preferences. Lifestyle changes, such as starting a family, moving to a different location, adopting new dietary habits, or even changing employment, can dramatically alter the products or services a customer might find appealing. Also, as your existing customer base ages, their needs and tastes will inevitably evolve. This aging demographic might prioritize comfort, convenience, or health-related products more than they did in their younger years. Therefore, understanding these changes and adjusting your products, services, or process is vital to remain relevant to existing and prospective customers.

The Decision to Adapt or Move

As a business owner, you're not obligated to cater to every change in demographics or customer tastes. Depending on your business model and the vision you hold for your company, you may find it more suitable to relocate your operations to an area whose demographics match your existing customer profile. Relocating could mean moving physically or focusing your online presence to better target your core customer group.

In other words, recognizing changes in customer preferences and community demographics isn't about automatically adjusting your business to suit them; it's about making informed decisions on the best course for your business. Awareness is essential here. Once you understand the changing landscape, you can decide whether to adapt and evolve alongside these changes or seek a different location or market that matches your established customer experience.

Should you choose to adapt and cater to the shifts in your community, continuing with a project that explores and addresses these changes will be the next step. Whatever path you choose, making these choices consciously is crucial, using the best information and insights available.

Recognizing these shifts in customer preferences and adapting is not just about staying relevant; it's about thriving in a constantly evolving business environment. Businesses that are active and responsive to their customer's needs are more likely to succeed in the long run. For instance, the bakery introducing a line of low calorie and gluten-free pastries could attract new customers while satisfying their existing customers' desire for healthier options. The bookstore that expands its e-book offerings could retain customers who might otherwise turn to online retailers. The grocery store that sources locally supports the local economy. Similarly, the apparel boutique that offers a broader range of sizes can cater to a more diverse customer base. In each case, you are not just reacting to change but proactively embracing it, turning challenges into opportunities for growth and expansion.

Step 2: Communicate

When you uncover your customers' needs, you must communicate these insights to your team and incorporate them into your marketing strategy. For instance, if your small online clothing store identifies a high demand for vibrant colors, communicate this finding to your team and strategize how to incorporate more colorful options into your product line.

Here is a sample script of how you can communicate the insights to any team members or interested parties.

"Team, our recent customer feedback shows an increased demand for low calorie baked goods. We can expand our offerings and cater to this growing market. As per our pastry chef, Jane, this will mean experimenting with new calorie-friendly recipes."

Step 3: Involve Your Team

Remember, your entire team, whether directly or indirectly, impacts the customer experience. Even if they don't interact face-to-face, their speed of response and efficiency in processing tasks can shape how customers perceive your business. Their input can be invaluable. For instance, your customer service representative might have noticed increased queries about a particular product type or feature.

Plus, your team is essential in implementing three simple tactics for gathering customer feedback: conducting customer surveys, monitoring social media, and analyzing customer purchase history.

Conducting customer surveys may involve a marketing person or people—internal or external, in creating and launching online polls on your social media page or website, asking your customers about their preferred products, services, or any other feedback you want to gather. To conduct customer surveys, you can create an online poll on your social media page or website asking your customers about their preferred products, services, or any other feedback you want to gather.

For example, a restaurant can ask customers about desired dishes, preferred cuisine types, and opinions on the restaurant's ambience.

Monitoring social media will require you or your customer service team member to actively check your pages and observe your customers' comments, messages, and reviews. Customer comments can provide valuable insights into their opinions and needs of your business.

For instance, a fitness studio can watch social media to discover popular workout trends among its customers and gather customer feedback on its services.

Analyzing customer purchase history can offer valuable insights into their buying behavior and preferences. You don't need a complex tool; look at your sales receipts and identify frequently purchased items and services.

For example, a pet store can analyze customers' purchase history to identify popular pet food types and frequently bought pet-related products among their customers.

Step 4: Provide Resources and Training

Equip your team with the necessary tools and training to gather and analyze customer feedback. Equipping your team could involve using a simple survey tool like Google Forms or training them on social media monitoring practices. In exploring customer purchase history, you'll need a reliable method of tracking sales data, which your data analyst can use to identify trends and patterns.

Set up keyword alerts: Be alerted when specific keywords related to your business on social media platforms are mentioned.

Regularly check customer feelings: This can help determine if the overall sentiment, or perception (what people think) about your business on social media, is positive, negative, or neutral.

Respond promptly: Quickly responding to customers' comments (within two to three days) or complaints (within one day) on social media shows you value their feedback.

Look for patterns: Do sales increase at certain times of the day, week, or year?

Compare periods: Comparing data from different periods can high-light trends. For example, comparing this month's sales to the same month last year can reveal growth trends.

Step 5: Refine and Adjust as Necessary

Don't be afraid to change your approach to getting feedback based on the results you receive. If your customers aren't responding to your online survey, consider trying a different approach, like a feedback box at your physical store, quick poll on your social media accounts, or question during checkout face-to-face, or online. For example:

Social Media Polls

Bookstore: "Which do you prefer, e-books or print books?"

Survey Examples

Clothing boutique: "What additional clothing sizes would you like us to carry?"

Step 6: Celebrate Success and Learn From Failure

Finally, celebrate every success, and view every failure as a learning opportunity. Whether you successfully launched a new product based on customer feedback or a marketing campaign didn't achieve the expected results, there are always lessons to be learned and applied in the future.

Celebrate Success

1. Organize a team lunch or outing to celebrate the successful implementation of a new strategy
2. Share customer feedback or positive reviews with your team

Common failures to look out for and how you can avoid them have been outlined as follows:

Don't misread customer information: Understanding customer information wrongly can lead to bad choices. Know your customer information well or get expert help.

How to avoid: Train your team to understand customer information correctly.

Ignoring negative feedback: Negative feedback can provide opportunities for improvement and ignoring it can lead to loss of customers.

How to avoid: Address negative feedback promptly and professionally, viewing it as an opportunity for improvement rather than criticism.

Lack of communication: If you don't adequately inform team members of changes or findings, it can lead to low morale and a poor customer experience.

How to avoid: Regular team meetings ensure that everyone has the same information and understands their role in implementing changes.

4.8 Finish: Prioritize Marketing and Business Personality for Rapid Expansion

The significance of prioritizing your business personality in your marketing strategy can't be overstated. Recognizing this vital aspect of your business could result in an incremental improvement that drives a 20+ percent increase in revenue. Therefore, investing your resources wisely to improve your business incrementally is paramount.

The central focus of this brief is to guide you through prioritizing your incremental improvement marketing efforts, helping you realize the best return on investment (ROI).

Objectives

This project aims to provide you with strategies for developing a business personality that matches your profitable customer's needs, evaluating ROIs, avoiding predatory marketing tactics, and prioritizing high-ROI marketing activities.

Scope

- Developing a strong business personality that reflects your values
- Ensuring sameness in the portrayal of your business personality across all marketing platforms

- Evaluating the ROI for various marketing and promotional expenses
- Identifying and avoiding predatory marketing tactics
- Prioritizing marketing tactics with a high ROI

Deliverables

- A defined business personality that is attractive to your profitable customers
- A consistent representation of your business personality across your website, social media profiles, physical retail properties, tools and systems, and all other marketing materials
- Clear goals and metrics for each marketing and promotional expense to measure its impact
- A prioritized list of marketing tactics that provide high ROI

Timeline

- Weeks 1 to 2: Develop business personality
- Weeks 3 to 4: Ensure consistency across all platforms
- Weeks 5 to 6: Evaluate ROI for marketing and promotional expenses
- Week 7: Identify and avoid predatory marketing tactics
- Week 8: Prioritize high-ROI marketing tactics

Resources Required

- Professional design services (optional)
- ROI tracking tools and analytics
- Marketing materials (signs, flyers, stickers, and product packaging)
- Access to marketing and promotional platforms (social media and e-mail marketing software)

Risks and Challenges

- Limited marketing knowledge and resources
- Potential predatory marketing tactics

- A gap between marketing expenses and business goals
- Difficulty maintaining sameness in business personality across platforms

Key Stakeholders

- Business owner
- Marketing person—internal or external
- Graphic designer—internal or external
- Web developer—internal or external

Step 1: Recognize the Need for Prioritizing Business Personality

As a small business owner, it's crucial to understand that focusing on your business personality can significantly impact your revenue, perhaps increasing it by more than 20 percent. But it's not just about a logo or specific colors. Your business personality encompasses the entire experience you provide to your customers.

This involves how you communicate, be it through e-mails or face-to-face interactions. It extends to the user experience on your website and the atmosphere of your physical location. Quality customer service is also a key component. How you resolve issues or handle complaints contributes to your business's overall image, affecting its trustworthiness and professionalism.

When customers have many options to meet their needs, the deciding factor often isn't just the product or service you offer. It's the complete experience with your business. A well-defined business personality can help you stand out, build trust, and encourage customers to return and tell their friends and family about your company.

Therefore, it's valuable to invest time in understanding and shaping your business personality. This isn't just about making a good impression; it's a long-term strategy for profitable growth.

Step 2: Communicate

Communication extends to how your business personality is reflected anywhere a current or potential customer might see it—online and offline. Ensure that your signage, vehicle, clothing or uniform, retail store, website, and social media profiles reflect your business personality and provide a positive and consistent customer experience.

An inconsistent business personality conveys a lack of professionalism and attention to detail, undermining the company's credibility and trustworthiness. Customers expect a cohesive and polished experience, and when inconsistencies arise in messaging or images they see, it raises doubts about the company's reliability and commitment to delivering a consistent product or service experience. By failing to establish a strong and consistent business personality, your company can become forgettable and struggle to be noticed when many people offer similar services or products.

Moreover, an inconsistent business personality hampers effective communication with customers and prospects. Inconsistencies in messaging across different platforms and touchpoints confuse potential customers, making it challenging to build a meaningful connection. Customers seek a consistent, coherent message that matches their needs and values. Inconsistent messaging can lead to misunderstandings, misinterpretations, and a disconnect between the company's promises and customers' perceptions. Without a reliable and genuine business personality, customer engagement and repeat business and word-of-mouth suffer, holding back the company's growth and success. Businesses must prioritize sameness and invest in maintaining a strong and cohesive business personality to build trust, establish a unique identity, and be attractive to potential and current profitable customers.

Ways to communicate your business personality improvements to customers and employees are as follows.

Customers

> *Script*: "Dear [Customer's name], we wanted to let you know that we have updated our social media profiles to reflect our business personality. We are now sharing valuable content tailored to your needs and interests. We encourage you to follow us on social media for the latest updates, promotions, and helpful tips. We value your engagement and look forward to connecting with you."

Employees or Stakeholders

> *Script*: "Team, we have recently undergone a marketing activity to improve our business personality and better connect with people who will most likely value and purchase our products or service. Our new messaging, images, and colors represent our values and the unique offerings of our business. As our valued team members, we thank you for consistently demonstrating our business personality in all customer interactions and communications. Together, we reinforce our uniqueness and build strong customer relationships."

Step 3: Involve Your Team

You need to involve your team to evaluate the ROI for your marketing efforts. Define clear goals and metrics for each marketing and promotional expense to measure its impact on your business.

Table 4.2 is a tool to help you in tracking marketing expenses. It breaks down different marketing methods such as social media advertising, e-mail marketing, local events, and direct mail campaigns. For each method, it sets specific goals such as gaining new followers or improving customer retention. It also lists metrics, which are the numbers you'll look at to see if you're reaching your goals. For example, if your goal is to gain 500 new followers on social media, the metric you'd look at is the number

Table 4.2 Example template for tracking marketing expenses

Marketing Expense	Goals	Metrics
Social media advertising	Increase business personality awareness; gain 500 new followers within the next quarter	Number of new followers; engagement rate
E-mail marketing	Improve customer retention; achieve a 10% increase in the open rate over the next quarter	Open rate; click-through rate; unsubscribe rate
Local events	Increase local business personality visibility; attract 100 attendees to sponsored community events	Event attendance; brand recognition
Direct mail campaign	Drive customer engagement; achieve a 5% response rate	Response rate; conversion rate

of new followers you get. This way, you and your team can clearly see what's working and what needs to be improved.

Together, analyze the results of each expense to see which ones generate the most ROI—specifically profitable revenue—track leads, sales, and other relevant metrics for your business. Thoroughly research the success of any marketing or promotion tactic, testimonies, customer success stories, to ensure it will generate more profitable customers rather than more customers who lose your money due to their needs or requirements that don't match your offering.

Step 4: Provide Resources and Training

To support your business personality development and marketing efforts, consider investing in professional strategy and design services such as consultants or strategists. These services can ensure that your marketing materials are of high quality and communicate your business personality effectively. Provide your team with the tools to track and analyze ROI, such as specific software or training.

Top five priority list of marketing tactics with a high ROI for service-based businesses:

Table 4.3 Example of marketing and business personality activities to prioritize for high ROI

Business Type	High ROI Marketing and Business Personality
Service-based businesses	• Consistent use of business personality* • Content marketing—demonstrate your expertise • Search engine optimization • E-mail marketing • Online review management • Referral or affiliate programs • Social media interaction is where profitable customers spend time online (not necessarily where you spend the most time on social media)
*	Consistent use of business personality includes images, logo image, colors, fonts, language, tone of voice, placement, how often you post or send anywhere the business is promoted: promotion for signs for the company, website, social media, printer flyers, stickers, and product packaging

Table 4.3 outlines the top marketing tactics that offer a high financial return for service-based businesses. Whether you're in retail, service-based, hospitality, creative, or professional services, there will be a priority for your business type. A common thread across all sectors is the consistent use of business personality elements such as images, logos, and tone of voice in various promotional channels. Beyond that, each business type has specific strategies that are more effective for them. For example, service-based businesses should focus on demonstrating expertise through content marketing. This table serves as a guide to help you learn to prioritize your marketing efforts for maximum impact.

Step 5: Refine and Adjust as Necessary

Regularly reevaluate and adjust your marketing expenses based on their financial return. Prioritize expenses with a clear and measurable result, such as targeted online advertising, search advertising, physical mail or e-mail marketing, or social media campaigns. Be cautious of marketing and promotional offers that seem too good to be true or pressure you into making a quick decision. Stay focused on your business goals and have a clear strategy.

Avoid being swayed by persuasive sales pitches, promises of instant success, or guilted into sponsoring a local community event, coupon book, or team for people who don't match your most profitable customers. Suppose you invest in expensive printing or collateral with a low return or pay for trade show booths, sponsorship, or speaking engagements not directed at your most profitable customers. In that case, it's time to reconsider or reduce these expenses.

Three Common Red Flag Warning Signs

Limited information, high-pressure sales, and unrealistic promises are three common red flags to look out for. For example:

> Limited information: Avoid marketing offers that provide little or vague information about their services or products. Legitimate marketing tactics should have clear and detailed information readily available.

Unaligned sponsorship or promotion requests: Exercise caution when approached with sponsorship requests from local community groups that do not align with your business goals. While supporting local sports teams or school events may initially appear appealing, assessing the potential return is crucial. Beware of requests primarily focusing on offering discounts or free products or services without providing tangible benefits contributing to your company's growth. Prioritizing sponsorships that have the potential to generate significant exposure or attract profitable customers is vital. By thoughtfully evaluating sponsorship opportunities, you can avoid guilt and ensure that you use your resources for events that benefit your company's growth. Following is a sample script to respond to sponsorship or promotional requests that don't agree with your business goals.

Script: Business owner: "Thank you for contacting us with the sponsorship request. We truly appreciate the work that local community group or school or organization does to support the community. While we understand the importance of these events, we must be mindful of how we allocate our resources to ensure the growth of our business."

Requester: "But we are a local organization and supporting us will show your commitment to the community!"

Business owner: "Absolutely, supporting the community is important to us. However, as a micro business, we have limited resources and need to focus on sponsorships that align more closely with our profitable customers, so we achieve our business goals. We believe in investing in initiatives that directly impact our growth and profitability. Is there any other way we can support your cause that meets our business objectives?"

This script allows you to politely decline sponsorship or promotional requests that do not align with your business objectives. By emphasizing the need to focus resources on initiatives that directly contribute to your growth while still expressing support and willingness to explore alternative ways of involvement, you can maintain positive relationships with the community while staying aligned with your business priorities and using limited resources in areas that have a high financial return—such as business personality and incremental innovation.

Learn from the activities that aren't bringing in the people who look like your most profitable customers and cancel those who do not provide the expected results. To make smarter decisions about where to invest your marketing dollars, use the following table to prioritize your expenses based on their ROI.

Table 4.4 Sample template for prioritizing expenses with clear ROI

Marketing Expense	ROI Calculation	ROI (%)	Priority
Social media advertising	(Gain from investment – Cost of investment)/Cost of investment		
E-mail marketing	(Gain from investment – Cost of investment)/Cost of investment		
Local events	(Gain from investment – Cost of investment)/Cost of investment		
Direct mail campaign	(Gain from investment – Cost of investment)/Cost of investment		

Table 4.4 serves as a sample template to help prioritize your marketing expenses based on their ROI. It breaks down different marketing activities such as social media advertising, e-mail marketing, local events, and direct mail campaigns. For each activity, it provides a formula to calculate financial return, which is the gain from the investment minus the cost, divided by the cost. By filling in these calculations, you can clearly see which marketing activities are most effective for your business. This allows you to focus your resources on high-impact activities and discontinue those that aren't delivering the expected results.

Here's a simple example to demonstrate how the return calculation works for a marketing tactic, using social media advertising as an example:

Example calculation for social media advertising financial return:

Cost of investment: You spent $100 on a Facebook ad campaign.
Gain from investment: You made $500 in sales from the ad.

Financial return calculation: Use the formula (Gain from investment – Cost of investment) divided by cost of investment.
($500 – $100) divided by $100
$400 divided by $100 equals 4

In this example, the return is 4 or 400 percent when turned into a percentage. This means you gained $4 for every $1 you spent on the campaign.

This simple calculation can help you understand the effectiveness of your marketing activities and guide you in making informed decisions.

Step 6: Celebrate Success and Learn From Failure

When your marketing efforts show a clear financial return, celebrate! Celebrate when you see the high return from targeted social media advertising, e-mail marketing, in-store promotions, loyalty programs, influencer marketing, or content marketing, demonstrating your expertise.

Celebrate Success

Customer testimonials: Post positive customer experiences on your website and social media pages. You can request feedback from happy customers and showcase their testimonials to celebrate your success.

Learn From Failure

Failures that often occur when prioritizing business personality occur for five reasons, copying competitors, chasing trends blindly, ignoring customer trends, inconsistent business personality, neglecting customer feedback, and neglecting long-term goals.

Copying competitors: Avoid the temptation to copy your competitors' business personalities. Focus on developing your unique business personality that represents your values and is relevant to people who will profitably buy your products or services.

You achieve success through continuous learning and adjustments. Keep refining your business personality and marketing strategy based on the return you see, and you'll be on the path to long-term success and growth.

Conclusion

We've covered how to keep growing and coming up with new ideas. But how do you price and manage expenses to make more money for your business? In the next chapter, "Maximizing Profitability," we'll look at smart ways to set prices and manage costs to make more money while staying true to your business. We'll also talk about how to measure your success and when it might be time to adjust your approach.

CHAPTER 5

Maximizing Profitability

Pricing and Cost Management Strategies for Small Businesses

Pricing your services correctly and managing costs effectively is crucial to your success. In this chapter, we'll share insights from real-life experiences and research to help you strike the right balance between pricing and cost management for maximum profitability.

In Section 5.1, we'll learn to set clear objectives for your pricing strategies. Understand your customers' willingness to pay and why they choose your business. We'll help you break down the pricing elements and prioritize the strategies that suit your business, like value-based and penetration pricing. Allocating your resources wisely and monitoring progress will be underlying themes here, as well as being flexible with the pricing models you adopt. In Section 5.2, we'll focus on managing your costs while keeping the customer experience at its best. We'll explore how you can negotiate with suppliers, reduce overheads, and potentially outsource noncore tasks. Section 5.3 will be a real-life example of how a small service company implemented the strategies discussed. We'll see how they initiated with clear goals, planned, and prioritized their actions, allocated resources effectively, and monitored progress.

In Section 5.4, I'll tie everything together, helping you evaluate what you've learned and how to take the next steps.

In addition, this chapter includes four project briefs, Sections 5.5 to 5.8, to increase your profits with simple cost-cutting techniques, discover your customers' value perception, streamline your businesses outsourcing, and negotiate better deals with suppliers.

These project briefs will provide practical tools and resources to increase profitability and manage costs more effectively.

5.1 Smart Pricing: Finding the Sweet Spot for Your Services

Welcome to Section 5.1, where we discuss the importance of pricing your services right. Understanding how to set prices is a vital aspect of marketing and can directly impact your business performance.

One of the critical factors to consider when setting prices is your customers' willingness to pay. Willingness to pay means understanding how much your customers will spend on your services and ensuring your prices match their expectations. For example, if you offer a high-end service, you may be able to charge a premium price, but if you cater to budget-conscious customers, you may need to price your services more conservatively.

Another essential factor to consider is identifying why people buy from your business, precisely the value they receive from your company versus your competitor. Knowing why customers choose your business can help set your high or low prices if customers understand the value your company provides.

Knowing what your competitors are charging is essential to setting your prices. Finding out what your competitors are doing helps you know how your prices compare and how your business is different. In addition, having a unique business personality that you consistently maintain will allow your business to charge prices that reflect your value and not push you into the spiral of competing on price, lowering it alongside competitors to keep customers while losing margin and profitability.

You can use several pricing strategies to maximize profits: value-based, penetration, or dynamic. Value-based pricing means setting your prices on the value of your services as perceived by your customers. In contrast, penetration pricing involves setting lower prices to gain market share and increase demand. Finally, dynamic pricing involves adjusting prices based on market demand and other external factors.

Pricing Strategies for Maximizing Profits

1. Value-based pricing
   What it is: You set your prices based on what your customers think your service or product is worth.

- In simple terms: If people really like what you do, you can charge more.
- Example: If you make handcrafted chairs and people are willing to pay extra because they love your unique design, that's value-based pricing.

2. Penetration pricing

What it is: You start by setting your prices low to attract more customers. Once you get a good customer base, you can slowly increase the price.

- In simple terms: It's like a "special intro offer" to get people in the door.
- Example: Think of a streaming service that offers the first month for just $1. Once you're hooked, the price goes back to normal.

3. Dynamic pricing

What it is: Your prices change based on different factors such as time of day, season, or how many people are buying.

- In simple terms: Prices go up when demand is high and go down when it's low.
- Example: A café that charges less for coffee during off-peak hours and more during busy times.

These strategies can help you earn more money while keeping your customers happy. The key is to know your customers and what they're willing to pay. Then, pick the strategy that fits your business best.

Here's a practical example to illustrate these concepts. A local bakery offers speciality cakes for events such as weddings and birthdays. But, first, they must consider their customers' willingness to pay to set prices right. Then, they can research what other local bakeries are charging for similar services.

To be unique, they focus on why customers choose them. The easiest way to find out why customers choose a company is by reading what they say in their reviews because, often, customers base their judgment on their comparison of your company with others they have used. For this example, customers choose them for their unique customized designs. Given the perceived value they offer their customers, they can reasonably charge a higher price for their services. However, they still need to consider their competitors' pricing to ensure they are not pricing themselves out of the market.

The bakery also monitors the latest trends in cake design and pricing, primarily by following competitors' social media; Instagram is good for visual images of designs and checking websites for what other bakers are charging. Based on this research, they decided to offer a range of prices, from lower-priced options for customers on a budget to higher-end options for customers who want a more customized cake design. They use value-based pricing to determine these prices, ensuring that their customers understand the value they offer.

Here is an example of a pricing strategy for a hair salon:

Hair salon: Focuses on value-based pricing, highlighting special skills such as trendy coloring. This lets you charge more for high-skill services. Your unique skills set you apart and let you demand higher prices. Add-ons can improve the customer's experience, warranting an extra fee.
- Basic cut: $20, just a simple haircut.
- Color treatment: $50, includes coloring your hair.
- Special style: $100, fancy hairdos or special treatments.

Pricing strategies can help you earn more money while keeping your customers coming back and recommending you to friends and family. The key is to know your customers and what they're willing to pay. Then, pick the strategy that fits your business best. It's crucial to understand that setting your prices high or low can be an effective approach if it aligns with a well-thought-out pricing strategy tailored to your customer experience. Simply mimicking your competitors' pricing, without understanding the "why" behind it, can backfire spectacularly. For instance, setting a low price that makes your service appear too cheap could deter rather than attract customers. Similarly, raising your prices just because everyone else is—without considering if your customer experience justifies it—can quickly alienate your customer base. The aim is not to match your competitors, but to understand your own business well enough to set the optimal price to match your overall experience at a profit.

5.2 Striking the Right Balance: Cost Reduction Versus Customer Experience

As a small business owner, managing costs is crucial for success. This section focuses on the role of cost reduction in small service businesses and offers practical advice for implementing these strategies without reducing the customer experience.

Identifying Areas for Cost Reduction

First, pinpoint areas where you can cut costs that won't negatively impact what customers expect from you. For instance, one option is to reduce overhead costs by moving to a smaller office, cosharing workspaces, working from home, or renegotiating your lease. You're not just saving on rent; you're also likely to cut down on utilities and maintenance.

Supplier Negotiations

Another angle is to negotiate better prices with suppliers. Consider bulk orders or seek out more cost-effective but equally reliable providers. Savings on material costs can then be reinvested in the business or even passed on to the customer in the form of value-added services or loyalty programs.

Outsourcing Noncore Tasks

You can also outsource tasks that are not at the heart of your business—such as accounting or marketing—to specialized service providers. The advantage here is twofold: it saves you on in-house staffing costs and allows you to focus on your core competencies. However, ensure that the outsourced service providers maintain the level of quality you require, as any shortfalls will reflect on your financial performance.

The Pitfalls of Cost Reduction

While cutting costs is tempting, it should never come at the expense of customer experience. For example, deep discounting because of an overall decline in your business might initially attract a lot of new customers, but these are often bargain hunters unlikely to return. Plus, existing clients might question the sudden drop in prices and wonder if it means a drop in quality.

Cutting corners on essential services or products is another risky move. If customers sense a decline in quality or service, they will likely take their business elsewhere. Therefore, the potential short-term gains from slashing prices are often not worth the long-term risk of losing loyal customers.

Balancing Act

The key to reducing costs effectively is to maintain the service quality your customers expect. When done thoughtfully, you can increase profitability without sacrificing the customer experience. You don't have to choose one over the other; it's entirely possible to be cost-efficient while still delivering value that keeps your customers coming back. The objective is to be smart about where and how you trim costs. A penny saved shouldn't be a customer lost.

For example, a small web design company could move to a smaller office and outsource accounting and marketing tasks. These cost-saving measures can help improve profitability while maintaining the customer experience.

The most common cost-cutting measures that reduce the customer experience are reduced staffing levels, outdated or insufficient equipment, inadequate training and development, inconsistent inventory management, neglected store, or office maintenance. For example:

Reduced staffing levels: Cutting back on staff can lead to reduced customer service and longer wait times. With fewer employees to assist customers, the overall experience may suffer, and customers may feel neglected or frustrated.

To make informed decisions on cost-cutting measures without compromising the customer experience, use customer feedback. This will help you understand what aspects of your service matter most to your customers. If, for example, fast response times are crucial to your customers, then reducing staff may not be the best place to cut costs.

Before implementing any significant cost-saving measures, consider a pilot test to assess the potential impact on customers. This step allows you to adjust if needed, ensuring that you're not jeopardizing the customer experience for short-term savings.

Always have a backup plan in place. If you find that a cost-cutting measure is negatively impacting the customer experience, you need to be prepared to reverse the changes quickly. Remember, it's easier to lose a customer than to gain one, and word of mouth, especially in the age of social media, can make or break your business.

While the focus here is on cost reduction, sometimes the key to a better customer experience is investment. Whether it's upgrading technology or providing staff with additional training, these investments can not only improve customer's staying and referring your business but can also lead to saving money in the long run.

A cost-effective way to keep customers is to create a customer loyalty or retention program. While this involves some upfront costs, the long-term benefits usually outweigh them. Loyalty or retention programs are likely to increase customer visits and sharing with friends and family, and low additional cost to you. Beware though that a program that focuses on discounts will only attract bargain hunters and potentially reduce your overall profitability.

Examples of what to include in a program that costs little but provides value to customers are thank you messages, birthday recognition, anniversary recognition, and first notice of limited stock or appointments. For example:

"Thank You" messages: Send customers simple, no-strings-attached "thank you" messages, showing gratitude for their choosing your business. The message could be as straightforward as, "We're delighted you chose us. Thank you for being our customer." Reminder: Avoid saying "thanks for supporting us" unless you're a charity, as the focus should be on the customer's choice to engage with your business because of the value it provides.

These tactics can significantly improve your customer retention strategy without adding significant costs.

In conclusion, cost reduction is essential for small service businesses, but it must not come at the expense of the customer experience. By carefully introducing cost-reduction strategies, always backed by customer feedback and testing, you can achieve a balance that increases profitability without reducing the level of service you promise customers. While some cost-cutting measures may be necessary, it's crucial to weigh these against the customer experience you've promised to deliver. The goal should always be to build a business that not only serves your customers well but also encourages them to keep coming back and recommending your company to other people. With careful planning of cost reduction methods, you can achieve long-term success.

5.3 Success in Action: A Small Service Firm's Journey to Master Pricing and Cost Management (Holiday Cottages)

This section will present the case study of a small vacation rental company that recognized the need to adapt to market changes to manage costs while effectively setting appealing and profitable prices. We will explore their specific steps to create a balanced approach to pricing and cost management, their strategies, and their impact on their business performance. I will also provide critical takeaways applicable to other small service companies.

Background of the company: The small service company we will examine is a holiday rental business operating for 15 years. A woman who identified a need for comfortable and affordable accommodation for short-term visitors to the Whitby area in North England started the company. With years of experience in the vacation rental industry, the owner was passionate about providing a welcoming customer experience and building a business she could be proud of.

Recognizing the need for change: After several years in business, the owner noticed changes in her local market. New holiday rental businesses were emerging, and some of her long-time customers were choosing these more recent properties. As a result, she was not getting as many bookings as her competitors and was reducing her prices to attract customers, which impacted her profitability. Also, some of her properties received negative reviews, prompting her to take action to remain appealing and continue growing her business.

Adapting to market changes: To respond to the changes in the local market, the owner consulted with friends and colleagues and met me. We first reviewed one of her properties and the business personality, identifying areas that could benefit from a balanced cost management and pricing approach.

After recognizing the importance of balancing pricing and cost management with continuous improvement to remain appealing and ensure long-term profitability, the business owner took the following steps to create a balanced approach.

They used online holiday rental websites to determine the prices people would pay for different types of accommodation in Whitby. They focused on analyzing higher priced competitors to understand how to compete within this pricing strategy.

They identified vital cost drivers, such as council tax, electricity, cleaning, sundries, mortgage, maintenance, bedding, crockery, dishes, and additional costs needed to adapt to market changes, such as online booking, increased payment options, Wi-Fi, and updated décor and furnishings. They determined the minimum price they could charge to cover their costs and make a profit.

Based on their market research and cost analysis, the holiday rental company made improvements to their service offerings and developed a pricing strategy that was appealing and more profitable. They increased their pricing for some properties and appealed to a broader range of customers, ensuring they met more customer needs while maximizing profits.

The holiday rental company offered more booking and payment options, improved the visual appeal by rearranging and minimizing décor, took more professional photographs, and created a business personality with messaging and pictures that met the emotional needs of prospective profitable customers. The changes they made attracted new customers without significant investment in property upgrades.

Results of the approach: The balanced pricing and cost management approach positively impacted the company's business performance. They attracted new customers and retained existing ones by implementing an appealing and profitable pricing strategy. They also increased their revenue by identifying key customer retention drivers, implementing cost-reduction strategies that didn't compromise customer experience, and raising prices to enhance overall profitability.

Key takeaways: As a small service company, you, too, can benefit from a balanced approach to pricing and cost management. You can achieve this by doing research, analyzing costs, making business improvements to remain relevant and appealing, and developing a pricing strategy that is profitable. In addition, nonmonetary incentives, such as a business personality that meets customers' emotional needs, can be used to attract new clients without incurring significant expenses. By following this approach, you can improve your business performance and profitability.

5.4 Effective Pricing and Cost Management: Key Insights and Next Steps

This section provided a comprehensive overview of pricing and cost management for small service businesses. We covered the importance of correctly pricing services and critical factors, such as understanding customer willingness to pay, identifying why customers buy from your business, and learning customer preferences. We also discussed pricing strategies such as value-based and penetration pricing to maximize profits. Furthermore, we examined practical cost reduction strategies, including reducing overhead costs, negotiating with suppliers, and outsourcing noncore activities.

The holiday rental case study illustrated a balanced pricing and cost management approach, allowing them to manage costs effectively while setting appealing and profitable prices. They achieved this by conducting market research, identifying why people choose their business, and regularly monitoring their pricing and cost management strategies against market changes. Their tactics included using a value-based pricing model and adding new service delivery methods to increase profitability. As a result, they significantly increased profitability while maintaining high customer satisfaction.

The key takeaways from this section are that proper pricing and efficient cost management are essential for running a successful service business. By understanding your customers, identifying why customers choose your business, and conducting regular market research, you can set appealing prices that attract and retain customers while maximizing profits. Moreover, implementing cost reduction strategies such as outsourcing noncore activities can help you lower overhead costs and improve profitability without reducing the customer experience.

To apply these insights, you should start by learning and understanding customer needs and willingness to pay. Next, analyze the space—virtual (website and social media) and physical (retail store, shop, center, and warehouse), that you provide services, pricing, and cost structures to identify areas for improvement, such as enhancing spaces to remain appealing or attract a broader range of customers, outsourcing noncore tasks, or renegotiating supplier contracts. Finally, you'll improve profitability and ensure long-term success by continuously monitoring and adjusting your services, pricing, and cost management strategies.

5.5 Start: Increase Your Profits With Simple Cost-Cutting Techniques

Reducing costs is a critical aspect of increasing profitability for small businesses. This project is vital as it introduces practical and simple cost-cutting strategies that can significantly improve profits without compromising the quality of products, services, or customer experience.

In this brief, we explore cost-cutting strategies across various areas of your business with an example for a retail business.

Objectives

The primary objective of this project is to provide you with practical and easy-to-implement cost-cutting strategies to enhance profitability.

Scope

- Identification of cost-cutting strategies
- Application of these strategies across different business sectors
- Exploration of free or low-cost resources to aid in cost reduction
- Consideration of the impact of these strategies on customer experience

Deliverables

- A comprehensive guide on cost-cutting strategies for small businesses
- A list of free or low-cost resources for each strategy

Timeline

- Weeks 1 to 2: Identification of cost-cutting strategies
- Weeks 3 to 4: Research free or low-cost resources
- Weeks 5 to 6: Selecting which strategies to implement
- Weeks 7 to 8: Implementation of cost-cutting strategies

Resources Required

- Research person for identifying cost-cutting strategies
- Business owner for approving strategies
- Business owner or team member for implementing measures

Risks and Challenges

- Identifying cost-cutting strategies that do not compromise promised product or service performance
- Finding reliable and affordable alternate resources or suppliers
- Ensuring the strategies apply to your business sector

Key Stakeholders

- Small business owner
- Business consultants (optional)
- Financial advisers (optional)

Step 1: Recognize the Need for Cutting Appropriate Costs

Reducing costs is vital to increasing your small business's profitability, and outsourcing tasks that aren't central to your business can help you save money and resources. As a small business owner, finding practical approaches to lower expenses is crucial without compromising the quality of your products, services, or customer experience. However, it's vital to avoid cost-cutting measures that could negatively impact customer experience, which include reducing product quality, cutting customer service, and eliminating value-added services. For example:

> Reducing product quality: While it might be tempting to use cheaper materials or processes, this can lead to a decrease in product quality, which can disappoint customers and harm your reputation.

Aside from avoiding these pitfalls, there are compelling reasons to undertake this cost-reduction project, such as cash flow management, resource allocation, competitive advantage, adaptability, customer retention, and decision making. For example:

> Cash flow management: Understanding how to cut costs effectively can lead to better cash flow, giving your business greater operational freedom and reducing financial stress.
>
> Resource allocation: A focused cost-reduction strategy allows for more effective allocation of limited resources, enabling you to invest more in areas that can stimulate growth, such as projects in this book and personalized plans for growth in the marketing strategy app.

So, doing this cost-cutting project isn't just about reducing expenses; it's about planning for the long-term benefit of your business. Doing this project is not an option but a necessity for improving profitability and growth. Knowing what and where to cut costs without damaging the customer experience is your first crucial step toward long-term success.

Step 2: Communicate

Effective communication with employees, interested parties, suppliers, and customers regarding cost-cutting measures is crucial. Crucial because misunderstandings or lack of information can lead to confusion, reduced morale, and even loss of valuable relationships. Clear, transparent conversations ensure everyone has the same information, minimizes negative impacts, and creates a sense of teamwork and respect.

> Employees: Explain the reasons for the cost-cutting measures and how they will help the company's financial health and sustainability. Assure them that their welfare is a priority. Sample script: "We are implementing cost-cutting measures to ensure our company's financial health. We value your contributions and will do our best to minimize any impact on your roles."
>
> Follow-up: Check in a week later to see how everyone is adjusting.
>
> Interested parties: Keep them informed about the changes and their reasons.
>
> Sample script: "We are taking steps to improve our financial health, which includes some cost-cutting measures. We believe these changes will make our business thrive in the long run."
>
> Follow-up: Send a monthly update summarizing the impact of the changes.
>
> Suppliers: Negotiate terms and ask for their understanding.
>
> Sample script: "Due to some financial adjustments, we are considering cost-cutting measures. We value our relationship and would like to discuss how we can continue our partnership in a mutually beneficial way."
>
> Follow-up: Share quarterly reports to update them on any changes that may affect them.
>
> Customers: Assure customers that you won't compromise the quality of products or services. Sample script: "We are implementing changes to improve efficiency. Rest assured, the quality of our products/services will remain our top priority."
>
> Follow-up: Conduct a short survey after a month to assess customer satisfaction.
>
> Share feedback: Here's how to provide your thoughts:
>
> Employees: Drop suggestions or questions into a box in the break room or send them through our usual channels.
>
> Interested parties: We'll set up a specific e-mail for your questions or suggestions.

Suppliers: We will designate a point person to handle your concerns and they will reach out soon.

Customers: We'll add a section on our website for your comments and questions about these changes.

Talking clearly with everyone involved is essential when you're cutting costs. Let your team, suppliers, and customers know what's happening and why. This helps avoid confusion and feelings of disrespect. It's also good to check in from time to time and ask what they think. This way, you can make changes if needed and keep things running smoothly.

Step 3: Involve Your Team

When outsourcing tasks, research providers carefully. Ask for recommendations from other business owners to find a proven reliable partner that delivers quality work or services. Ask your team for ideas: Your employees know their jobs well. Ask for their input on how to save money or improve processes.

When implementing new technology, train yourself and your employees properly to make the most of new tools. Check the work: Have someone review new purchases or outsourced work.

When looking for a reliable supplier, consider the following:

1. Quality assurance: The supplier should have a strong track record for quality and consistency.
2. Timely delivery: They should be able to deliver goods on time, as delays can disrupt your operations.
3. Good communication: They should be easy to contact and quick to reply.
4. Compatibility: Make sure you can work well together.

Red Flags to Avoid

1. Poor reviews or references: Negative feedback from other customers is a significant warning sign. Watch for warning signs: Negative reviews or not being open should make you reconsider.

2. Lack of transparency: If the supplier is not open about their processes or business practices, this could indicate potential issues. Have an exit strategy: Discuss how you can end the partnership if needed.
3. Inconsistent pricing: If the supplier's pricing is conflicting or unclear, it could lead to unexpected costs. If their prices keep changing, be cautious.

Safety first: Before fully committing, start with a smaller project to evaluate their performance.
Backup supplier: Keep contact information for an alternate supplier.
Regular check-ins: Keep an eye on how the supplier is performing.

Involving your team is more than just a good idea; it's essential for getting the most out of your cost-saving strategies. From seeking team input to smartly picking suppliers, each step you take should be a team effort. Be careful, be open, and always have a plan B. Keep an eye on how things are going and be ready to make changes if you need to. This way, you're not just saving money—you're also building a stronger business.

Step 4: Provide Resources and Training

Making smart choices in resources and training will help you achieve both efficiency and effectiveness in your business operations. This step goes beyond just cutting costs; it's about investing wisely in tools and education that can dramatically improve how your business performs over time. In the following, we look at strategies tailored for different types of businesses, showing you how to use free or low-cost resources effectively. Whether it's using online platforms for retail sales or managing inventory, knowing where to put your time and money can make all the difference.

Use free or low-cost resources such as freelancer marketplaces or online project management tools to simplify the outsourcing process and improve efficiency. To prioritize cost reductions, consider areas where you can cut costs without negatively impacting your customer experience. Start with the expenses significantly affecting your expense statement and work down the list.

Here are the top 10 items or expenses that typically don't impact the customer experience and can be cut or reduced or outsourced:

1. Office space
2. Office supplies
3. Utilities
4. Nonessential travel
5. Advertising in low-financial return channels
6. Unproductive staff
7. Unused software subscriptions
8. Expensive professional services
9. Overstocked inventory
10. Nonessential training or events

Following is a potential strategy for a retail business.

Retail Business

Strategy 1: Sell products online using platforms such as Amazon or Etsy to avoid the costs of owning or renting a physical store. Free or low-cost resources such as Shopify, Wix, or square offer easy-to-use online store platforms with various pricing plans.

Strategy 2: Use a just-in-time inventory system to reduce storage costs and the need to store large amounts of inventory. Google Sheets is a free tool for tracking inventory levels and orders.

Strategy 3: Use a third-party logistics provider to manage shipping and warehousing. Check at least three to see which offers the pricing plans that meet your needs.

By following a cost-reduction strategy, you can improve your profits, save money on hiring and training staff, buy equipment, and maintain office space, all while maintaining a positive customer experience.

Step 5: Refine and Adjust as Necessary

Running a business is not a set-it-and-forget-it operation, especially when you're aiming to be smart about costs. You've involved your team, communicated openly, and chosen good tools and training. Now, it's time to keep an eye on how these choices are affecting both your profit and your day-to-day operations.

Keep talking to your team members, suppliers, and customers. Are your cost-cutting measures working as planned, without harming service quality or customer experience? If something's not working, don't hesitate to make changes. For example, if a new supplier isn't living up to their promises, it may be time to renegotiate or look elsewhere. Or if customers are complaining about a new change, it might be worth revisiting your approach.

It's also important to look back at your own notes or meeting records to see what you originally planned. Sometimes the busy-ness of running a business can make us forget why we made certain decisions in the first place.

Lastly, carefully review your spending every couple of weeks. Sit down and go over your budget. Does everything match your goals? Are there new opportunities for smart spending or further cuts that won't hurt your business?

Don't be too hard on yourself if you need to make changes. Every change is a learning opportunity that brings you closer to running a smarter, more efficient business. Keep refining and adjusting as needed.

Step 6: Celebrate Success and Learn From Failure

Cost-reduction strategies can help you reduce expenses while increasing profitability, all without compromising the quality of your customer experience, products, or services. Prioritizing your cost-cutting and outsourcing tasks that aren't your core business frees up your time to focus on growth.

Celebrating Success

It's crucial to recognize and celebrate your wins. This could be as simple as a mention in a team meeting, or more substantial like a small bonus or pay rise for everyone. If your cost-cutting led to substantial savings, share this good news with your team. For example, if the new shipping strategy saved the company $2,000 this month, consider distributing a portion of that as a one-time bonus. This not only rewards the team but also reinforces the importance of cost-saving measures.

Learning From Mistakes

However, not all cost-cutting measures will be successful, and that's okay. Common pitfalls to look out for include lowered product quality, sagging employee morale, and losing customers. For example, if your decision to switch to a cheaper supplier resulted in delays and customer complaints, acknowledge the mistake, and consider switching back or finding an alternative. Make sure your team is well-supported and informed throughout these adjustments to minimize negative impacts.

By celebrating your wins and learning from any setbacks, you keep the team motivated and focused, smoothing the way for future success.

5.6 Plan: Discover Your Customers' Value Perception Through Easy Market Research

This project is crucial as it aims to help you understand your customers' preferences and willingness to pay for your products or services. By implementing the steps outlined in this project, you can make informed pricing decisions, leading to increased profitability and success.

In this brief, we explore the process of conducting simple market research to understand customer value perception and how to apply the insights gained to improve business operations and profitability.

Objectives

The primary objective of this project is to guide you in conducting effective market research to understand your customers' value perception and apply the insights to make informed pricing and service decisions.

Scope

- Choosing a method to collect customer feedback
- Creating an effective survey or questionnaire

- Sharing the study with customers
- Analyzing the information gathered
- Applying the insights to improve business operations

Deliverables

- A comprehensive guide on conducting market research
- A template for creating effective surveys
- Strategies for sharing surveys and encouraging customer participation
- Techniques for analyzing customer feedback
- Recommendations for applying the insights gained

Timeline

- Weeks 1 to 2: Choosing a method to collect customer feedback
- Weeks 3 to 4: Creating and testing the survey
- Weeks 5 to 6: Sharing the survey with customers
- Weeks 7 to 8: Analyzing the information gathered
- Weeks 9 to 10: Applying the insights to improve business operations

Resources Required

- Market research tools (e.g., Google Forms, SurveyMonkey)
- Social media platforms for sharing surveys
- Incentives to encourage customer participation
- Time and a person to analyze the feedback and apply the insights

Risks and Challenges

- Customers participating in your survey
- Misinterpretation of customer feedback
- Resistance to change within the business
- Time and resource constraints

Key Stakeholders

- Business owner
- Marketing person (optional—internal or external)
- Sales team (optional—internal or contract)
- Customer service team (optional—internal or contract)
- Customers

Step 1: Recognize the Need for Knowing Customer Preferences

Understanding your customers' preferences and willingness to pay for your products or services is the key to a successful business. Knowing what your customers truly value gives you a competitive edge, enabling you to tailor your products and service more effectively. This gives you an advantage because you know what your customers want better than your competitors do. It's not just about offering a product or service; it's about providing the right ones that match your customer's needs and want, at the right price. This understanding is not stationary but changes with time, market trends, and customer expectations. Therefore, recognizing the need for this project is the first step toward matching your business offerings with your customers' value perception, which is crucial for making informed pricing decisions.

For instance, if you run a restaurant and discover through your research that your customers highly value smaller portions, you might decide to design smaller or shared portion menu options and reflect this in your pricing.

In your case, understanding your customers' preferences allows you to make better pricing decisions, leading to increased profitability and a more successful business.

Step 2: Communicate

It's essential to communicate the importance of this project to your team, as the team's active participation will significantly contribute to its success. When everyone on the team understands why this project is important, they'll put in more effort. Plus, your team members are the ones who talk to customers and handle the products and services, so their input can make a real difference. If the team isn't part of the project to understand customer preferences, they might not want to make the changes the research suggests. This can lead to problems with the new ideas or even people not wanting to try them, which goes against the goal of getting ahead of the competition.

Explain to your team the process of collecting customer feedback and how this information will help the business make informed decisions. Make them understand that their role in this process is operational and strategic, as the insights gained from the feedback will shape the business's future direction.

For instance, you could tell your team,

> We're starting on a project to understand better our customers' preferences and willingness to pay for our [products and or services]. We'll collect feedback through online surveys, social media polls, and direct conversations. Your role in this is crucial, as the information we gather will help us make better decisions about our pricing and offerings. Please participate and share any insights you may have.

Similarly, it's essential to communicate with your customers about this project. Let customers know that their feedback is valuable, and you will consider it when improving products or services. Communicating with customers makes them feel valued and more likely to participate in your surveys or feedback sessions.

For example, you could tell your customers, "Hello! Would you like better products and services from us? We have upcoming surveys. Your answers will help us improve what you get from us. Will you join?" When the survey is ready, send something like this: "Hello, you can now let us know what products or services you'd like. By taking a minute to answer, you're helping us improve what you receive from us. This means better products and services for you. Thank you!"

Talking clearly with your team and customers is very important for this project. Your team needs to know that their role is important for making better business choices. Customers should know that their answers in the survey will help us give them better products and services. Good communication helps everyone understand what you are doing and why it matters. This makes the project work better and helps your business grow.

Step 3: Involve Your Team

Involving your team, even if it's a small one or consists of contractors, in creating a survey or questionnaire is a strategic move that can offer multiple benefits. Those who interact directly with customers, whether part-time employees, contractors, or even family members helping, often have valuable insights into customer preferences and behavior. They can contribute meaningful questions to the survey, enhancing its effectiveness.

For example, someone who handles sales or customer interactions might suggest questions about the purchasing process or customer service experience. Suppose you have a contractor who helps with product development or service delivery. In that case, they might propose questions about the product features or aspects of the service that customers value the most.

Involving your team in the process also promotes a sense of ownership and inclusion. When team members participate in creating the survey, they are more likely to understand and support the changes that result from customer feedback. They will see first-hand how customer insights can lead to improvements in the business, making them more likely to implement these changes.

Moreover, testing the survey with a few customers before sharing it with others is a good practice. Your team members can help identify any confusing questions or technical issues. They can also help interpret the feedback from these initial responses, which can be used to refine the survey before it is distributed more widely.

In essence, involving your team in this step not only improves the quality of your survey but also creates an attitude of making customer-based decisions within your business, where everyone understands the relevance of customer feedback and is committed to improving the company with it.

Step 4: Provide Resources and Training

In this crucial step, we will discuss the practical aspects of conducting market research, from choosing a method to collect customer feedback to understanding the information gathered. I'll provide a detailed example, illustrating how to create, distribute, and analyze surveys and apply the insights gained to improve business operations.

Choose a method to collect customer feedback.

Provide resources such as market research tools and training on using them effectively. Depending on your business type, you might choose online surveys using free tools such as Google Forms or SurveyMonkey, social media polls on Facebook, Twitter, Instagram, WhatsApp, Signal, or other messaging apps with customers, or in-person conversations or phone calls.

Create a simple survey or questionnaire.

Keep it short and use simple language that your profitable customers will understand. Use existing templates and questions from survey tools to avoid confusing questions. Include open-ended questions or ones that provide a box for customers to type comments to understand why customers have their opinion, so you have helpful information to improve. Test your survey with a few customers before sharing it with others.

Share your survey with customers.

Sharing could be through e-mail, social media, or in-person interactions. Offer incentives, like a gift with purchase, to encourage customers to participate. For example, a restaurant business could create a social media poll asking: "On a scale of 1 to 5, how likely are you to recommend our value money menu items?" Or "Do you prefer smaller or larger portion sizes?" and share the poll on their social media accounts.

Analyze the information you gather.

Pay attention to repeating trends in your customers' answers. Their preferences will help you learn what your customers like and how much they will pay for your products or services. Look for ideas that come up several times in the responses you collect. For instance, if at least five people mention they love your unique flavors, it could mean your special recipes are a strong selling point. If more than half of the respondents say they'd pay extra for a faster delivery option, it might be worth offering express shipping for an additional fee. If several customers mention that they appreciate your friendly customer service, it's a good sign that you should continue prioritizing excellent communication with your clients.

Here is an example of how you could apply these steps to a restaurant business:

Restaurant business: Create a social media poll asking: "On a scale of 1 to 5, how likely are you to recommend our [value money menu items]? Or "Do you prefer [smaller portions] or [larger portions]?" Put in what you are asking inside the brackets [x]. Share the poll on your social media pages and use the insights to adjust menu pricing or portion sizes.

Step 5: Refine and Adjust as Necessary

Refine and adjust your business operations based on the feedback received. Refining could involve adjusting your prices, improving your services, or changing your product offerings to meet your customers' needs. Refining and adjusting your business operations based on feedback is a continuous process. It's important to stay attentive to signs that further refinement or adjustment is needed. Five signs to look out for include decreased sales, negative customer feedback, increased customer complaints, declining repeat business, and low survey response rates. For example:

Decreased sales: If you notice a decrease in sales after adjusting your prices, it might indicate that customers do not perceive the value of your product or service to be equivalent to the new price. In this case, you may need to refine your pricing strategy, perhaps by offering tiered pricing, bundles, or long-term contracts.

Remember, the goal of refining and adjusting based on feedback is to meet your customers' needs better and improve your business's profitability. It's a process of continuous improvement, so stay open, willing to make changes as necessary.

Step 6: Celebrate Success and Learn From Failure

Celebrate the success of understanding your customers' value perception and making informed business decisions.

Celebrating success is an essential part of any project. It increases morale and reinforces the value of the work done. One way to celebrate the success of this project is by sharing the positive changes that resulted from it with your team. Sharing could be in the form of a meeting where you discuss the improvements made, the increase in customer happiness, or the rise in sales or profitability. Another way to celebrate is by acknowledging the efforts of everyone involved. Acknowledgment could be a simple thank you note, a small celebration, or even a reward for those who played vital roles in the project.

However, not all aspects of the project may go as planned, and it's equally important to learn from these failures or challenges. Three common failures in projects like this to look out for include low response rates, inconsistent or inconclusive data, no improvement in business metrics. For example:

> Low response rate: If you're not getting enough responses to your surveys or feedback requests to make decisions with, it could be a sign that customers are not engaged, the survey method is not practical, or customers don't know how to respond. To fix this, you could try different ways of distribution, offer incentives for participation, or make the survey shorter and easier to complete.

Remember, both successes and failures provide valuable learning opportunities. When you celebrate success and learn from failures, you will continuously improve your market research efforts and make more informed decisions for your business.

5.7 Do: Streamline Your Business by Outsourcing Nonessential Tasks

This project is paramount as it seeks to explore the benefits and strategies for outsourcing noncore activities to specialized service providers. By delegating tasks that don't directly impact your core competencies, you can focus on your primary business objectives, leading to increased efficiency, productivity, and cost savings.

In this brief, we explore the process of identifying, prioritizing, and outsourcing noncore activities in a way that does not compromise the customer experience.

Objectives

To guide small businesses in identifying, prioritizing, and outsourcing noncore activities to specialized service providers without compromising the customer experience.

Scope

- Identification of noncore activities
- Prioritization of noncore activities for outsourcing
- Selection of suitable outsourcing suppliers
- Effective communication with potential suppliers
- Negotiation of terms and conditions with suppliers

Deliverables

- A comprehensive list of noncore activities ideal for outsourcing
- A prioritized list of actions to outsource based on business performance and profitability
- A list of potential outsourcing suppliers
- A guide on how to communicate effectively with suppliers
- A template for negotiating terms and conditions with suppliers

Timeline

- Weeks 1 to 2: Identification and prioritization of noncore activities
- Weeks 3 to 4: Research and selection of potential outsourcing suppliers
- Weeks 5 to 6: Communication and negotiation with selected suppliers
- Weeks 7 to 8: Finalization of agreements and initiation of outsourcing

Resources Required

- Dedicated team for project implementation
- Access to online directories and industry associations for supplier research
- Legal advice for contract negotiation and finalization

Risks and Challenges

- Identifying the right tasks to outsource
- Finding reliable and cost-effective suppliers
- Ensuring clear and effective communication with suppliers
- Negotiating favorable terms and conditions

Key Stakeholders

- Business owners
- Project implementation team
- Potential outsourcing suppliers
- Legal advisers

Step 1: Recognize the Need for Outsourcing Noncore Activities

You might be wondering if outsourcing is a common practice among businesses. The answer is a resounding yes. A survey conducted by Deloitte reveals that approximately 60 percent of companies have adopted outsourcing as a strategy to manage noncore activities. Research indicates that outsourcing is a trend and a strategic decision made by over half of businesses.

Moreover, outsourcing isn't just common; it's also highly beneficial. A study by Accenture found that a staggering 89 percent of businesses that have outsourced noncore activities are satisfied with their decision. These businesses have seen not only a clear, positive impact on their operations but also their profit.

Outsourcing information technology (IT) services is one of the key areas where businesses have seen substantial benefits. According to a report by PwC, companies that have outsourced their IT services have experienced an average cost savings of around 14 percent. Over 10 percent is a significant saving, especially for businesses where every dollar counts.

These statistics underscore the potential benefits of outsourcing noncore activities. As a business owner, recognizing the need for this project could be your first step toward achieving cost savings, increasing satisfaction, and making a positive impact on your business.

Step 2: Communicate

Once you've recognized the need for outsourcing, the next crucial step is to communicate this decision effectively. Communicate with your employees, family members involved in the business, customers, and other interested parties. Clear and transparent communication is vital in ensuring that everyone understands the reasons behind the decision and the benefits it will bring to the business.

Communicating With Employees

Your employees may feel anxious or uncertain about the decision to outsource. It's important to reassure them about their roles and explain how outsourcing can help the business grow and become more efficient.

Sample Script

> We want to share some important news about an important deci-sion to outsource some of our noncore activities. We decided to become more efficient so we can focus more on what we do best. We want to reassure you that this decision is not about replacing you but enhancing our capabilities and attractiveness.

Communicating With Family Members

If you have family members involved in your business, they may have emotional as well as financial investments in the business. It's essential to explain the reasons behind the decision and show how it will benefit the company in the long run. Include statistics and revenue projections to make the benefits of your decision compelling and factual. If available, seek an expert's verification of your statistics to support any stubborn family members opposed to change. Provide a clear summary of what it means, specifically benefits, for the family members involved to reduce potential pushback on change.

Sample Script

> We've decided to outsource some noncore activities. After careful consideration, we decided to focus more on our core competencies. We believe this will help us grow by [xx] percent, or $[xx] in [period] revenue and become more profitable within [x] period.

Communicating With Customers

Your customers may have concerns about how outsourcing might alter your products or service quality. Ensuring customers know your decision, aims to enhance the quality and efficiency of your services.

Sample Script

> We're making some changes to improve our services. We've decided to outsource some of our noncore activities, allowing us to focus more on providing you with the most appropriate products or services. We're confident that this decision will help your experience as a customer.

Communicating With Other Interested Parties

Other interested parties, such as investors or partners, will be interested in the strategic implications of outsourcing. Be prepared to explain how outsourcing will improve efficiency, reduce costs, and enhance focus on core competencies.

Sample Script

> We've decided to outsource some noncore activities. This decision will allow us to focus more on our core competencies, improve profitability by [x percent], and reduce costs by [x percent]. We believe this will enhance our appeal and drive our growth in the long term.

Remember, clear and effective communication is critical when implementing changes in your business. By addressing any concerns and highlighting the benefits, you can ensure a smooth transition to outsourcing.

Step 3: Involve Your Team

Talk with your team to identify your noncore activities. Make a list of all the tasks that are not related to your core business activities and consider outsourcing them. These may include administrative tasks, marketing, accounting, customer experience, and IT support. Next, determine which activities a third-party provider can do more efficiently and cost-effectively. Once you have identified the noncore activities to outsource with your team, you need to find and select your outsourcing suppliers.

Here are some tips to share with your team for communicating effectively what can be outsourced and securing suitable suppliers:

Involving your team in identifying noncore tasks to outsource is a strategic move that can free up time and resources for everyone. Team members often have a ground-level view of daily operations and can pinpoint tasks that are necessary but not necessarily the best use of in-house talent. Open, transparent communication is key here. You can hold a team meeting or a brainstorming session to discuss this openly.

Sample Script

> Hey team, as we grow, we want to make sure we're all focusing on what we do best. I'd love to hear your thoughts on tasks that are important but don't necessarily need to be done by us. Don't worry, this isn't about cutting jobs; it's about making our workflow more efficient so we can achieve more.

By taking this approach, you not only gain valuable insights but also make your team feel valued and included. This can lead to increased participation, without causing undue stress among your team members.

Research and compare different suppliers: Use online directories, referrals from other businesses, or industry associations to find potential outsourcing suppliers. Compare their services, reputation, and pricing to find the best fit for your business.

Communicate your needs clearly: When approaching potential suppliers, be clear about your requirements and expectations. Provide a detailed description of the tasks you want to outsource, the timeline, and other relevant information.

Ask for references: Ask potential suppliers for previous client references to confirm their experience and reliability. Contact these references and ask about their experience working with the supplier.

Negotiate the terms: After choosing a supplier, negotiate the terms of the agreement, including details of work, pricing, and timeline. Ensure that you get everything in writing, including a service level agreement (SLA).

Step 4: Provide Resources and Training

Prioritize the noncore activities based on their impact on your business performance and profitability. For example, you may want to prioritize outsourcing accounting and bookkeeping to a specialized service provider since these activities can be time-consuming and require technical knowledge. On the other hand, keep customer experience in-house since it can help you build better customer relationships.

Once you have identified the noncore activities to outsource, you need to find and select your outsourcing suppliers. When approaching suppliers, have clear expectations and communicate effectively to ensure they understand your needs and goals. Build a solid supplier relationship for a smooth and successful outsourcing experience.

Here is an example of how to approach an accounting and bookkeeping supplier:

Accounting and bookkeeping approach: Contact an accounting and bookkeeping service provider specializing in small businesses. What to say:

Hi, I'm a small business owner, and I'm looking to outsource my accounting and bookkeeping tasks. I need help managing my financial records, preparing tax returns, and ensuring compliance with regulations. Can you provide these services, and what is your pricing?

Outsourcing noncore activities can be an excellent way for you to save time and money and improve your business performance. By identifying which activities are noncore, prioritizing them, and finding suitable suppliers to outsource to, you can free up your time, people, and funds to focus on your business's core functions to increase profits and deliver the promised customer experience.

Step 5: Refine and Adjust as Necessary

Outsourcing noncore activities is an excellent way to save time and money and improve your business performance. However, it's important to remember that outsourcing relationships may need to be refined and adjusted over time to ensure they continue to meet your business needs.

You might need to refine and adjust based on the quality of the work, communication, and cost effectiveness. For example:

Quality of work: One of the key things to monitor in an outsourcing relationship is the quality of work delivered. If you notice a decline in quality or the work is not meeting your expectations, it may be time to refine the relationship. Refining could involve providing more detailed instructions, adjusting the scope of work, or even reconsidering the supplier if the quality does not improve.

What to look for: Regularly review the work delivered. Look for errors, delays, or signs that the work is not up to your standards. Pay attention to customer feedback and whether it has changed for the better or worse after the change.

Remember, the goal of outsourcing is to help your business become more efficient and effective. Regularly reviewing and adjusting your outsourcing relationships can ensure that they continue to support this goal.

Step 6: Celebrate Success and Learn From Failure

Celebrate each successful step in outsourcing, whether through a virtual appreciation event, sharing your success story, or creating a reward program for your team. For example:

> Virtual appreciation event: Organize a virtual meeting or party with your team and the outsourced supplier to celebrate the project's success. Hold a virtual event using video conferencing tools such as Zoom or Google Meet. During the event, you can highlight the project's achievements, share positive feedback, and express gratitude to everyone involved. Gratitude celebrates success and strengthens the relationship with your supplier.

Learn from common failures such as poor communication, lack of quality control, and not defining clear goals and expectations from the start. For example:

> Poor communication: One of the most common failures in outsourcing projects is poor communication. A lack of good communication can cause misunderstandings, delays, and poor-quality or incorrect work. Establish clear communication channels and regular check-ins with your outsourced supplier to avoid this. Make sure both parties clearly understand all expectations and requirements.

Outsourcing can be intimidating, but it can be a seamless and positive experience for your business with the proper steps, tips, and tools.

5.8 Finish: Strengthen Your Bottom Line by Negotiating Better Deals With Suppliers

Renegotiating supplier contracts is vital for the success of small businesses. It allows for better pricing and terms, improving profitability and long-term growth. This project gives you the necessary knowledge and skills to effectively renegotiate supplier contracts, so you secure more favorable agreements and increase your profitability.

In this brief, we explore the step-by-step process of renegotiating supplier contracts using clear communication, thorough preparation, and collaborative negotiation strategies. By following these steps, you can maximize your chances of securing better pricing and terms from your suppliers.

Objectives

- Equip you with the knowledge and skills to renegotiate supplier contracts effectively
- Help you secure better pricing and terms, leading to enhanced profitability
- Create respectful relationships with suppliers for long-term success

Scope

- Focuses on renegotiating existing supplier contracts rather than establishing new ones
- Guides reviewing current contracts, preparing for negotiations, and effectively communicating desired changes
- Emphasizes the importance of compromise and maintaining positive relationships with suppliers

Deliverables

- Understanding the critical areas, you can negotiate in supplier contracts
- Strategies for effective communication during negotiations
- Tips on preparing for negotiations, including researching industry and competition
- Examples of clear and concise articulation of desired changes
- Guidance on being open to compromise and finding mutually beneficial solutions
- Insights on avoiding unreasonable demands that may harm supplier relationships

Timeline

- The duration of the renegotiation process will depend on individual circumstances and complexities
- Allocate sufficient time for reviewing contracts, preparing for negotiations, and engaging in constructive discussions with suppliers

Resources Required

- Access to current supplier contracts and associated documentation
- Research materials, such as industry reports, trade publications, and online resources
- Time for reviewing contracts, conducting research, and scheduling meetings with suppliers
- Effective communication channels such as e-mail, phone, or online video calls to engage with suppliers

Risks and Challenges

- Suppliers may be unwilling to negotiate certain aspects of the contract
- Limited resources and team members may pose challenges in conducting research and negotiations
- Unreasonable demands or strained relationships

Key Stakeholders

- Small business owner(s) or managers
- Supplier representatives
- Team members or contractors
- Customers

Step 1: Recognize the Need for Renegotiating Contracts

Renegotiating supplier contracts is essential for small businesses' success as it allows for better pricing and terms. Recognizing the need to review and improve supplier agreements periodically can enhance your profitability and ensure long-term growth. This project will equip you with the knowledge and skills to renegotiate supplier contracts successfully.

Supplier landscapes are ever-changing, influenced by market trends, competition, and economic conditions. Sticking with the same supplier for an extended period without renegotiating can result in missed opportunities for better terms or pricing. Suppliers may offer new clients attractive deals that aren't extended to existing customers. Therefore, it's crucial to keep an eye on the market and be open to renegotiating contracts to ensure you're not overspending.

Prices are not static; they fluctuate due to various factors such as demand, supply chain disruptions, or inflation. Regularly reviewing market prices for the goods or services you're sourcing can provide you with the weight needed during renegotiations. Tools such as price comparison platforms or industry reports can be invaluable in this regard. Make sure you're not just settling for what you're currently paying when you could be getting a better deal.

Beyond pricing, there are other elements in a supplier contract that may need revisiting, such as delivery timelines, payment terms, or quality standards. Periodic renegotiation is not just about cost-saving; it's also about improving every aspect of your supplier relationship. This proactive approach ensures that the contract matches your business goals and adapts to any changes in your operational needs or market conditions.

By doing this project, you can create a more cost-effective, efficient, and adaptive operation, better positioning your business for long-term growth.

Step 2: Communicate

Effective communication plays a crucial role in the renegotiation of supplier contracts. Clearly stating your desired changes in pricing or terms during negotiations is essential. Expressing gratitude for the supplier's services and maintaining a positive tone throughout the negotiation process is necessary. Communicate your reasons for renegotiating and the changes you want, ensuring the supplier understands your business's needs.

Schedule a meeting with your supplier. Contact your supplier to schedule an appointment to discuss renegotiating your contract. Again, be honest about your reasons for renegotiating and the changes you want.

Tip: Always start the conversation positively, expressing gratitude for the supplier's services and your relationship.

Clearly articulate what you want. During the meeting, clearly say what you want, including specific pricing or term changes. Then, explain why these changes are essential for your business.

Here is an example of how to clearly state what you want and explain why the changes are essential for your business during a meeting to renegotiate a service supplier contract:

Service contract renegotiation: "We're happy with your service and want to reduce overhead costs. We want to discuss renegotiating our contract to reflect more favorable terms, such as a longer payment schedule or reduced fees. Is this something you'd be willing to consider?" or "We're looking to reduce our overhead costs, and we believe that we can achieve this by renegotiating the terms of our contract. Specifically, we would like to see a reduction in the fees charged for your services. We believe this is important for our business as it will help us improve our profitability and invest in other areas of our business. By reducing our overhead costs, we'll be able to allocate more resources toward our marketing and sales efforts, which will ultimately help us to grow our business."

In this example, the business owner clearly states what they want, including specific pricing or term changes, and explains why these changes are essential for their business. By doing so, you can make a strong case for why your supplier should agree to your proposed changes and increase your chances of reaching a mutually beneficial agreement.

Tip: Use data to back up your requests. Show the supplier how much you currently spend, how much you would save with the proposed changes, and how much more you might spend in the future as a result.

Be willing to compromise. Negotiation is a give-and-take process, so be willing to compromise. For example, be open to alternative pricing or term changes and be ready to make concessions if necessary.

Here is an example of being open to alternative pricing or term changes and making concessions if necessary:

If a supplier cannot meet your desired price point, you may need to negotiate alternative terms, such as a more extended payment schedule or a lower volume commitment.

Remember, negotiation is a give-and-take process. Be willing to listen to your supplier's concerns and suggestions and open to alternative solutions that benefit both parties.

It's crucial to know when to inform your customers about changes in supplier contracts. Transparency is a foundation of customer trust, so you'll want to notify them when changes directly impact their experience or costs. This could be a significant improvement in product quality, a change to more sustainable sourcing, or a necessary adjustment in pricing. In these instances, customers have an interest in the changes and should be made aware to maintain a transparent and trusting relationship.

However, not all changes require customer communication. If the alterations in your supplier contracts don't directly affect the customer—such as internal adjustments to payment terms or a supplier switch that doesn't impact product quality or pricing—these can be kept within the company.

Step 3: Involve Your Team

While you may have limited team members or rely on contractors, involving them in renegotiation can provide valuable insights and support. Talk with team members who have knowledge of the supplier relationships or can contribute to the negotiation strategy.

Beyond that, consider the skill sets within your team. For instance, someone with strong analytical skills could be tasked with researching market trends and competitor pricing. Those with legal backgrounds or contract management experience can review the fine print and suggest protective clauses.

Additionally, team members who are directly involved in using the supplied goods or services can offer practical perspectives on quality, reliability, and areas for improvement. Their hands-on experience can be a crucial asset in understanding the real-world implications of any changes in the supplier contract.

By actively involving your team in various aspects of the renegotiation process, you not only make more informed decisions but also create a sense of ownership and responsibility. This approach can lead to better contract terms and a stronger, more unified team.

Before renegotiating, review your current supplier contracts to understand the terms, pricing, and expiration dates. Then, identify areas where you can secure better pricing or terms and where you want to see changes made through doing research, yourself, or with the help of a team member.

When reviewing your current supplier contracts, there are several aspects that you can negotiate, such as pricing, payment terms, delivery schedule, quality control, volume discounts, length of contract, and termination clauses. For example:

Pricing: Pricing is one of the most common areas businesses try to renegotiate. You can negotiate lower prices for the products or services you purchase, especially if you have been a loyal customer or can commit to purchasing larger volumes.

Remember, not all aspects of a contract will be negotiable, and some suppliers may be more willing to negotiate than others. Therefore, it's vital to approach negotiations respectfully to find a solution for both parties.

Tip: Look for areas where you can offer value to the supplier in exchange for better pricing or terms. Terms could be a longer term commitment, more frequent orders, or a larger volume.

Prepare for the negotiation. Research the supplier's industry and competition to understand their pricing and what they offer. Determine the maximum amount you will pay or the minimum terms you are ready to accept.

Step 4: Provide Resources and Training

To strengthen your negotiation skills and improve the outcome of supplier contract renegotiations, consider providing resources and training to yourself and your team. Research the supplier's industry and competition to understand pricing and offerings. Additional information will give you the confidence to negotiate effectively. Plus, have your current spending, potential savings, and future spending with the proposed changes on hand, reinforcing your position during negotiations.

Here is an example of how to prepare for a negotiation by researching the supplier's industry and competition:

> If you are negotiating with a service provider, research the pricing and services offered by other providers in the same industry. Compare their services and prices with those of your current provider. This information will help you understand what a fair price is for the services you need and what other options you have available.
>
> In today's globalized market, the options for service providers are more extensive than ever. The Internet has made it possible to source services from around the world, giving you a broader range of choices and competitive pricing. This global reach means you're not limited to local or even national providers; you can explore international options that may offer better terms or specialized services that better meet your business needs. By considering providers from various regions, you can use these global options to get a better deal during talks.
>
> Tip: Gather information from free or low-cost online resources such as industry reports, trade publications, or government data.
>
> Here is a summary example action plan for a small business wanting to renegotiate supplier contracts.
>
> Objective: Secure better pricing or terms with suppliers to achieve cost savings.
>
> 1. Contract analysis (two weeks): Examine existing contracts, identify areas for negotiation, and create a checklist for market research. Goal: Complete within two weeks.

2. Market research (four weeks): Investigate current market rates and find alternative suppliers. Goal: Finish in four weeks.

3. Negotiation strategy (one week): Develop a strategy, including areas to focus on during negotiation. Goal: Finalize within one week of market research completion.

4. Negotiate with suppliers (two weeks): Use the strategy to negotiate with current suppliers and be open to counterproposals. Goal: Wrap up in two weeks.

5. Evaluate alternatives (two weeks): Compare current suppliers to alternative options in terms of pricing or terms. Goal: Decide within two weeks.

6. Contract finalization (one week): Either sign new contracts with alternative suppliers or adjust existing ones based on negotiation outcomes. Goal: Conclude within one week of deciding.

Budget

- 120 hours of team effort spread across three months
- Potential legal fees: $500

Step 5: Refine and Adjust as Necessary

Throughout the renegotiation process, it is crucial to refine and adjust your strategies as necessary continuously. Monitor the progress of the renegotiations and be open to compromise and alternative solutions. If your specific demands are not met, consider exploring other benefits that may contribute to a mutually beneficial agreement or source an alternate supplier that will meet your demands. Maintain a flexible approach and be willing to adapt to changing circumstances.

Tip: Always keep the long-term relationship in mind. Avoid making unreasonable demands that could damage the supplier relationship. However, it's equally important not to compromise your business needs just to maintain a relationship. If other suppliers offer better terms, don't hesitate to make a change; being taken advantage of is not the basis for a healthy, long-term partnership. It's not uncommon for micro business owners to develop friendships with their suppliers. While personal relationships are valuable, they shouldn't deter you from renegotiating or even changing suppliers if it's in the best interest of your business. Failing to do so could ultimately harm your profitability.

Unreasonable demands that could damage the supplier relationship include demanding much later payment, requesting a significant price reduction, or threatening to take your business elsewhere. For example:

Requesting a significant price reduction: If you ask your supplier to reduce their prices by 50 percent without any justification or evidence, this unreasonable demand is unlikely to be met.

In general, it's essential to approach negotiations with your suppliers respectfully. Avoid making unreasonable demands that may harm the relationship and be open to compromise and finding a mutually beneficial solution. If all else fails, find new suppliers.

Step 6: Celebrate Success and Learn From Failure

Once you successfully finish supplier contract renegotiations, take a moment to celebrate the positive results. Recognize the value of securing better pricing and terms contributing to your business's growth and profitability. Celebrate with public recognition, team lunch, or document the success story to share publicly. For example:

> Public recognition: After successfully renegotiating a contract, publicly recognize the team members involved. Recognition could occur during a team meeting, in a company newsletter, or on your business's social media platforms. It's a great way to acknowledge the hard work and dedication that went into the negotiation process.

Plus, take the opportunity to reflect on any challenges or failures encountered during the process. Learn from these experiences and use them as valuable lessons for future supplier negotiations.

Avoid common failures of lack of preparation, poor communication, or not being open to compromise. For example:

> Lack of preparation: Not being prepared is one of the most common failures in contract renegotiation. Failure includes not fully understanding the current contract, not researching market rates, and

not having a clear goal for the renegotiation. To avoid this, ensure that you thoroughly prepare before entering renegotiations.

In summary, renegotiating supplier contracts is a valuable way to secure better pricing and terms for your business. Review your current agreements and research options, approach your suppliers clearly and concisely, and be open to compromise. Use the tips for negotiating with suppliers and the examples provided to communicate more effectively and secure suitable suppliers. Finally, always keep a positive and respectful tone during the negotiation process.

Remember, renegotiating supplier contracts is an ongoing process that requires consistent effort and effective communication. Follow the steps provided to confidently complete the renegotiation process and maximize the benefits for your business.

Conclusion

You've learned how to make more money while keeping your business true to itself. So, what should you remember and what's your next move? The last chapter will sum it all up. I'll go over the main points from each chapter and give you a simple plan to put what you've learned into action. I'll also share some resources for further learning and tips for staying on track.

CHAPTER 6

Conclusion

Congratulations on completing this book! Reading through each chapter taught you essential strategies for profitable growth in your small business. In addition, these recommendations are backed by scientific research, so you know they're tried and tested.

In Chapter 1, we learned the importance of creating and maintaining a consistent business personality. Chapter 2 taught us how to recognize and embrace change, while Chapter 3 focused on making your business personality visible. Chapter 4 covered continuous improvement and innovation, and Chapter 5 discussed pricing and cost management.

Remember, doing these recommendations is not a one-time event, but consistent implementation will help you achieve sustainable success in your business. Following the steps outlined in this book, you no longer need to be confused about building and growing a profitable business.

Now it's time to put what you've learned into action. Develop a clear business personality that is attractive to your profitable customers, train your employees to demonstrate your business values, protect and enhance your business personality, embrace change, and prioritize marketing and business personality for rapid expansion.

Following this guide, you can build a strong, recognizable, and profitable business personality for your small business. Ultimately, you'll create a company with a strong foundation that will help you achieve your goals much better knowing what to focus on to achieve success as a small service company.

6.1 Business Personality Importance Highlights

A business personality is how a business interacts with customers, influences customer perceptions, looks, acts, sounds, and behaves, and makes decisions within the customer experience. A strong business personality increases a company's attractiveness, establishes credibility and trust with potential customers, sets your business apart from the rest when there are lots of people offering the same type of products or services, and builds a base of customers who return regularly and tell their friends and family. It also attracts high-quality employees and helps the company recover from setbacks or negative publicity.

Developing a strong business personality involves creating a distinct identity for the business that customers can easily recognize. A business personality includes elements such as a logo, benefit slogan, color scheme, consistent image, tone of voice and language in social media posts, signage, uniforms, layout, and process in a physical business setting. Clear objectives are essential to guide these efforts and ensure that they match the business's goals. A professional online presence, an understanding of customer values, and a specific customer experience are also crucial elements of a strong business personality.

A solid business personality can significantly contribute to financial success when many people offer similar services or products by 20 percent. Investing time and resources into business personality allows you to stand out from competitors and attract potential customers. However, when many people sell similar products or services, it may also be necessary to focus on other aspects of the company, such as improving product or service quality. In conclusion, building a strong business personality is a vital strategy for small business success, and breaking tasks down and prioritizing can make this process more manageable and effective.

A consistent business personality, which represents the business's messaging and promise, builds customer trust, and creates a memorable business personality. Consistency can be achieved by defining the business's personality messaging and promise, and ensuring everything a customer can see or hear about your company matches the business personality online or in real life.

Consistency in business personality is crucial for businesses with single or multiple locations or franchises. Each site should follow the same guidelines to maintain sameness and ensure a consistent customer experience. Companies that fail to maintain a consistent business personality can confuse customers and harm their reputation. In conclusion, creating and maintaining a consistent business personality is essential for building customer trust and creating a memorable business personality.

The "Start-Plan-Do-Finish" framework offers you a structured approach to crafting a compelling business personality. You begin with research to pinpoint unique market opportunities, followed by detailed planning to clearly define your business's personality. The focus then shifts to execution, emphasizing the significance of fulfilling your business's personality promise to customers. The chapter concludes by highlighting the importance of a consistent online presence in solidifying your business personality. This comprehensive guide serves as your roadmap to navigate the complexities of establishing and maintaining a distinct and effective business personality.

6.2 Embracing Change Highlights

Recognizing and embracing change is vital for businesses to stay relevant. Recognition involves monitoring the external and internal environment of your business for signs of change, such as new or different competitors, declining sales, or customer feedback, and managing these changes on a project basis. Clear goals and objectives are crucial when starting a project, as they provide focus and increase the likelihood of success. Research shows that small business owners who operate in an uncertain environment are more likely to focus on business personality activities, which can significantly increase financial performance.

When rapid changes occur in the local market within a year, it's an indicator that businesses should focus on their business personality and improve their services to stay relevant. Ignoring these changes or pretending they won't impact the business environment can result in missed growth opportunities. Prioritizing business personality from the start is essential as it shows how your businesses is different from competitors, builds customer relationships and trust, and reduces focus on price when choosing a service company during a changing business environment. It's essential because in times of change customers want consistency. Businesses can recognize changes in their environment by the intensity and difference of changes occurring from one year to the next.

Once you identify the need to adapt to changing times, it's crucial to start making changes. Consistency in business personality across all marketing materials is essential for success, and you should communicate service improvements to the local market.

Treating the business personality as a vital asset is crucial, as it is the most critical asset of a successful company and can add value when selling the business.

By setting clear objectives and frequently improving service delivery to adapt to changing consumer preferences, companies can effectively recognize and embrace change. Recognizing and embracing change is essential for growth and success.

Recognizing the right time to start adapting to change is crucial for you. Waiting too long or making changes too quickly without proper planning can result in poor business performance compared to competitors.

The right time to start is when changes in the local market are intense, continuous, and significant within a year, regardless of the company's age, size, or competition level. Breaking down a change and growth project into smaller tasks is an effective project management principle to avoid feeling overwhelmed and focus on one task at a time.

Monitoring progress and adjusting the plan is crucial. Measuring sales, customer feedback, and employee performance helps track progress and make necessary adjustments. You should remain adaptable and prepared for future changes by continuously monitoring the local market and planning accordingly.

Creating a customer experience strategy that matches your business's promise is crucial for small businesses. This strategy helps improve services, increase customer loyalty, and drive business growth. To create an effective strategy, you must recognize the need to know your customers and define profitable customer segments. By understanding your profitable customer's preferences, you can provide an experience that meets their expectations and attract similar customers.

Involving your team, including employees and yourself as the owner or manager, is essential. Encourage employees to share customer-related experiences and suggestions based on their interactions. Refining and adjusting the customer experience strategy is an ongoing process. Implement changes based on customer feedback and measure their impact on metrics such as CES, NPS, repeat business, and online reviews. Celebrate successes and acknowledge improvements to motivate your team and learn from failures to refine and enhance the customer experience continuously. By following these steps, small businesses can develop a customer experience strategy that represents their values and drives business growth.

In Chapter 2, the focus is on embracing change to ensure that your business remains competitive and relevant. The "Start" phase emphasizes recognizing signs of change in your business environment and setting clear objectives. The "Plan" phase delves into how to prioritize your business personality and create a roadmap for change. "Do" is all about action—implementing the changes, focusing on consistency in your business personality, and developing a customer experience strategy. Finally, the "Finish" phase involves monitoring the impact of these changes through key performance indicators such as sales and customer feedback. By breaking down the process into these manageable steps, you can navigate the complexities of change more effectively.

In summary, the right time to start adapting to change is when changes in the local market are intense, continuous, and significant within a year. You can initiate and manage change effectively by starting with a plan, communicating with employees, monitoring progress, staying adaptable, and seeking expert advice when needed.

6.3 Visibility for Success Highlights

To stay visible and attract customers, you must make service and experience improvements and effectively communicate them. The first step is recognizing areas where you've made changes to enhance your services or business environment. Take time to list these improvements and share them with your customers. You can mention updates to your website, added features such as online booking or chat support, and even physical changes such as freshening up your store.

After identifying the improvements, develop a communication plan using your already known effective ways to communicate with customers— via e-mail, text, private message, telephone, mail, social media, or your website. ChatGPT, an AI language model, can assist you in crafting messages to convey the benefits of these improvements clearly and concisely. Share the news with your customers using the chosen communication methods and measure the impact through customer engagement and sales. It's also essential to involve your team, ensuring everyone understands the improvements and can share them well.

Providing the necessary resources and training to do any new improvements effectively is crucial. Resources can include technical tools or informative materials. Monitor the impact of the announcements and refine them as necessary. Celebrate successes and learn from failures, treating them as opportunities for growth. By consistently identifying areas of improvement, communicating effectively, and maintaining a customer-centric approach, you can enhance your business personality and continuously improve the customer experience.

Protecting and enhancing your business personality is paramount for your company's success. One crucial step is trademark registration, which gives you exclusive rights to use your business name and symbol. Registration protects your identity and ensures that others can't use anything similar. Maintaining a positive online presence is also vital. Regularly monitoring platforms such as your website, social media profiles, and review websites allows you to address any negative feedback promptly. By responding to customers and showing you care, you build trust and maintain a good reputation.

Consistency across all channels is vital. Whether it's your website, social media, or in-store displays, representing your business personality consistently reinforces your business identity and makes it easily recognizable to customers. Also, enhancing your business personality involves providing a relevant customer experience.

Providing customers with what you promise creates customers who return and tell others about your business and improves your financial performance. By striving for consistency, registering your trademark, monitoring your online presence, and focusing on customer experience, you can protect and enhance your business personality, ensuring its strength and value into the future.

6.4 Continuous Growth Highlights

Enhancing customer experience is crucial for you to build a good reputation, retain customers, and ensure business success. Incremental improvements in how a business is run significantly impact the customer experience and financial performance. You need to continuously improve your services to increase customer retention and improve ratings.

You should announce any changes and improvements to your services. By sharing these updates through existing channels such as websites, social media, e-mail, mail, or telephone, companies can keep customers informed and build confidence in their ability to meet evolving needs.

Customer preferences and expectations change over time, influenced by market trends and competitors. It's essential to gather customer feedback through surveys or reviews and use that information to make necessary changes and improvements. Training employees in effective communication and problem-solving skills is also crucial.

Offering ways for customers to give feedback, such as online review platforms or suggestion boxes, can provide valuable insights for improvement. Small service businesses can embrace incremental improvement by conducting market research, brainstorming, and evaluating ideas, testing new concepts, and staying committed to continuous improvement. You can improve your products and services by updating yourself with market trends and customer preferences and remaining relevant.

Overall, incremental improvement is essential for small service businesses to enhance customer experience, meet changing customer needs, and improve business financial performance by 17 percent. Businesses can thrive in a dynamic business environment by prioritizing customer feedback, making small changes over time, and committing to ongoing improvement.

6.5 Maximizing Profitability Highlights

It is vital to price your services correctly. A critical aspect of this pricing is understanding the customer's willingness to pay and the value they perceive in your products, services, and overall customer experience. This understanding helps set prices that meet customer expectations and your business goals.

The three pricing strategies discussed were value-based, penetration, and dynamic pricing. With value-based pricing, you set your prices on the customer-perceived value of your services. This strategy is particularly effective when a business offers a unique service or product that customers highly value.

Penetration pricing involves setting lower prices to gain market share and increase demand. This strategy is often used by new businesses when many people offer similar services or products, aiming to attract customers with lower prices and retain them with high-quality services.

Dynamic pricing involves adjusting prices based on market demand and other external factors. Dynamic pricing strategy is commonly used in industries where demand fluctuates, such as hospitality or online stores. It allows businesses to maximize profits during peak demand periods and maintain sales during off-peak times.

Identifying why customers choose a particular business over competitors and understanding competitor pricing are crucial factors in setting prices. A company with a unique personality and promise statement can set prices that reflect its value, avoiding competing on price and maintaining profitability.

Setting prices correctly is vital to maximizing profits and improving business performance. By understanding customer expectations, applying appropriate pricing strategies, and considering competitor pricing, businesses can set prices, contributing to their success and sustainability.

It is crucial to reduce costs without compromising the customer experience. Critical areas for cost-cutting include reducing overhead costs by downsizing office space, renegotiating leases, or outsourcing noncore tasks such as accounting or marketing to external providers. However, cost reduction should never precede customer experience, which could lead to losing existing clients.

Standard cost-cutting measures that could potentially reduce the customer experience include reduced staffing levels, outdated or insufficient equipment, inadequate training and development, inconsistent inventory management, and neglected store or office maintenance. It's crucial to carefully assess cost reduction strategies and consider their potential impact on the customer experience. While cost-cutting measures are sometimes necessary, you should balance them with maintaining an appropriate customer experience.

In conclusion, cost reduction is vital for small service businesses, but it should never compromise the customer experience. By carefully starting cost-reduction strategies, you can increase profitability and achieve long-term success. The key is to strike the right balance between reducing costs and maintaining the right customer experience.

6.6 Reflecting on Success Stories

Throughout this book, we have explored several success stories that embody the principles discussed in each chapter. These stories demonstrate how small business owners have achieved remarkable results by applying the strategies and tactics presented. Let's recap some of these success stories and the key takeaways for you.

In one case study, a small cleaning company focused on developing a strong and recognizable business personality. By showing how they are unique from competitors and making necessary changes to their business personality, the company experienced a significant increase in new customers and retention of existing ones. The key takeaways from this story include staying aware of the local market and competition, building a distinct business personality, and using social media to announce improvements.

Another success story featured a hair salon that successfully adapted to market changes. The owner prioritized understanding her customer base, improving her business environment, and diversifying services. By starting these strategies and using online marketing channels more effectively, the salon experienced a remarkable increase in customers and continued growth.

A piano tuner also found success by improving and increasing the visibility of their business personality. Through analysis, creating a new business personality, and a consistent online presence, the company attracted new customers and achieved financial goals. This story highlights the importance of adapting to market changes and demonstrating superiority through a strong business personality.

The small animal care clinic succeeded by continuously improving and adapting its services. By understanding the preferences of pet owners in their community and adjusting their approach, they built trust and interest, resulting in attracting more customers and revenue.

Lastly, a vacation rental company thrived by adapting to market changes and mastering pricing and cost management. The company attracted new customers and increased revenue through market research, service improvements, and a relevant pricing strategy.

These success stories demonstrate the significance of critical principles for micro business owners. These include staying aware of the market, building a strong and distinct business personality, adapting to changes, using online channels, continuously improving services and physical business spaces, and starting effective pricing and cost management strategies. Each company's story illustrated the importance of setting clear goals, planning, prioritizing actions, allocating resources effectively, and maintaining flexibility and effective communication throughout the process.

By applying these principles and learning from these success stories, you can achieve growth and success in your venture.

6.7 Next Steps and Action Plan

It's time to act and implement the critical strategies you have learned from this book in your business. Following the steps and procedures discussed in each chapter, you can set yourself up for growth and success. Here is guidance on how to proceed and an action plan to help you.

Start at Chapter 1: Revisiting Chapter 1, where you learned about understanding your business personality and identifying who will profitably purchase your products and services. Review the project briefs provided within the chapter to assess your current business personality and how it represents your goals. Adjust and improve to ensure that your business personality is attractive to people most likely to purchase your services or products by including customer feedback in any improvements to your business.

Prioritize resources: As you move through each chapter, prioritize your resources effectively. With limited resources, focus on the strategies most impacting your growth by tracking metrics that matter to customers, such as their effort and loyalty. Refer to the project briefs within each chapter to identify the projects that match your business goals and allocate your resources accordingly.

Training and learning: Embrace the idea of continuous learning and improvement. Use any training opportunities and resources available to you. Whether it's attending workshops, webinars, or online courses, invest in your development and get, outsource, or hire the necessary skills and knowledge to grow your business. Use technology to simplify your business processes to improve the overall customer experience.

Adaptation and flexibility: Stay aware of market changes and be open to tweak your strategies accordingly. Regularly assess the effectiveness of your business personality, marketing efforts, and customer experience. Ensure that your business remains compliant with changing laws and regulations by consulting legal advice. Adjust as needed to ensure that you remain relevant and attractive in your industry. Refer to the project briefs in relevant chapters to guide you in adapting and refining your approach.

Celebrating success: Celebrate your achievements along the way. Recognize and acknowledge the milestones you reach and the growth you experience. Use these moments as motivation to continue pushing forward and striving for further success. Celebrate with your team, customers, and friend and family supporters, and share your success stories through your marketing channels to enhance your business personality.

By following these steps and starting the strategies discussed in each chapter, you can make significant progress in improving your business and achieving similar success to the case study business owners. Remember, you don't have to figure it out on your own. The actionable projects and guidance provided within each chapter are designed to support you in maximizing your limited resources and setting achievable goals. Act, stay committed, and embrace the process of growing your business one step at a time.

6.8 Further Resources

For further resources and expert advice on a marketing strategy that emphasizes incremental innovation and avoids blindly copying other businesses, consider the following options:

Marketing Strategy App by Stratagease: Available on the Google Play and Apple App Store. This App offers a comprehensive toolkit for developing and executing an effective marketing strategy.

Developed by Dr. Raewyn Sleeman, marketing strategy expert, and author of this book, this app gives valuable insights and actionable steps personalized to your business needs. With user-friendly features and expert guidance, you can define your unique business personality, implement incremental innovations, and access a wide range of resources with little or no marketing knowledge or experience. Using the Stratagease app, you develop a marketing strategy that drives success simply, quickly, and affordably. As a special offer for readers of this book, you will receive one-month free use of the App, without any ads, to raise your understanding and action of the concepts presented.

Marketing consultants and agencies: Seek guidance from experienced marketing consultants or agencies specializing in small businesses or your industry. These professionals can give expert advice tailored to your unique challenges and goals, helping you develop a marketing strategy that incorporates incremental innovation and attracts the right customers.

Industry-specific publications and blogs: Explore industry-specific publications, blogs, and websites offering insightful articles, case studies, and expert tips on marketing strategies. Consider participating in online courses, webinars, and industry networking events to gain hands-on experience. Find sources focusing on incremental innovation and giving practical advice for small business owners. These resources can provide valuable inspiration and keep you up-to-date with the latest trends and strategies in your industry.

When seeking expert advice, find resources that match with your business values and objectives. Avoid relying solely on group social media discussions or generic advice. Embrace the incremental innovation approach discussed in this book and use expert resources to develop a personalized marketing strategy for your business so its uniqueness is evident to existing and prospective profitable customers and promotes healthy growth.

You will create an effective business growth strategy by combining the foundational strategies and tactics outlined in this book with the abovementioned resources.

About the Author

Dr. Raewyn Sleeman is a distinguished business strategist, a marketing expert, and an educator passionate about helping small businesses succeed. With a rich professional background spanning diverse industries, she has led teams to create impactful marketing campaigns and drive growth through innovative marketing strategies.

Dr. Sleeman holds a doctorate in Business Administration from Athabasca University, where her research focused on branding (business personality) and innovation in small service companies. Plus, she earned an MBA (with Merit) from the University of Liverpool and a Bachelor of Commerce and Management from the University of Auckland. She is also a Fellow of the Higher Education Association with a Postgraduate Certificate in Learning and Teaching (PGCLT) through BPP University.

As a management lecturer at QA, Dr. Sleeman teaches apprenticeship courses on business, digital technology, change, innovation, and project quality management. While a management lecturer at BPP Group, Dr. Sleeman taught master's level courses and served as a module leader for marketing, digital transformation, innovation, change, technology, and business. Her expansive teaching style and ability to simplify complex concepts stem from her experience overcoming dyslexia and a speech impediment at a young age.

Throughout her career, Dr. Sleeman has held various senior positions in marketing and communications, including founding Stratagease Technology Corporation. Her dedication to giving back to the community is evident through her extensive volunteer work with organizations such as HTB Shelter, Life Support, and Union Gospel Mission.

Dr. Sleeman's numerous accolades include being shortlisted for The Governor General's Gold Medal Award and being nominated for the RBC Canadian Women Entrepreneur Awards multiple times. In addition, Dr. Sleeman enjoys golfing, gardening, and painting when she's not working.

In this groundbreaking book, Dr. Sleeman shares her wealth of knowledge and experience, providing small business owners with practical tools and insights to achieve sustainable growth and success.

Index

**OTHER TITLES IN THE PORTFOLIO AND
PROJECT MANAGEMENT COLLECTION**

Kam Jugdev, Athabasca University, Editor

- *The Professional Project Manager* by Carsten Laugesen
- *The Agile Enterprise* by David Asch
- *Power Skills That Lead to Exceptional Performance* by Neal Whitten
- *A Project Sponsor's Warp-Speed Guide* by Yogi Schulz and Jocelyn Lapointe
- *Great Meetings Build Great Teams* by Rich Maltzman and Jim Stewart
- *When Graduation's Over, Learning Begins* by Roger Forsgren
- *Project Control Methods and Best Practices* by Yakubu Olawale
- *Managing Projects With PMBOK 7* by James W. Marion and Tracey Richardson
- *Shields Up* by Gregory J. Skulmoski
- *Greatness in Construction History* by Sherif Hashem
- *The Inner Building Blocks* by Abhishek Rai
- *Project Profitability* by Reginald Tomas Lee

Concise and Applied Business Books

The Collection listed above is one of 30 business subject collections that Business Expert Press has grown to make BEP a premiere publisher of print and digital books. Our concise and applied books are for...

- Professionals and Practitioners
- Faculty who adopt our books for courses
- Librarians who know that BEP's Digital Libraries are a unique way to offer students ebooks to download, not restricted with any digital rights management
- Executive Training Course Leaders
- Business Seminar Organizers

Business Expert Press books are for anyone who needs to dig deeper on business ideas, goals, and solutions to everyday problems. Whether one print book, one ebook, or buying a digital library of 110 ebooks, we remain the affordable and smart way to be business smart. For more information, please visit www.businessexpertpress.com, or contact sales@businessexpertpress.com.

www.ingramcontent.com/pod-product-compliance
Lightning Source LLC
Chambersburg PA
CBHW061148220326
41599CB00025B/4397